To Marcus & Hilda

May you both be filled with comfort & joy

In Her Own Words

as you read

The After-death Journal of Princess Diana

of Dina's Journeys

Many blessings

through

Chris Toomey

Christine Toomey

1-2-03

edited by

Tony Stubbs

English Rose Press

In Her Own Words

The After-death Journal of Princess Diana
through Christine Toomey
edited by Tony Stubbs

Published 2000
Copyright © 1999 Christine Toomey

03 02 01 00   0 9 8 7 6 5 4 3 2 1

Published by
ENGLISH ROSE PRESS
PO BOX 2669
MT. PLEASANT, SC 29465

www.englishrosepress.com

ISBN: 0-9675961-3-0
Printed in the United States of America

Contents

Acknowledgments iv

Dedication v

Introduction vi

Editor's Note xiii

1:     Waking Up 1

2:     Exile on Pebble Island 19

3:     The Level of Healing 33

4:     Onwards and Upwards 43

5:     The Level of Mirrors 55

6:     The Level of Tears 71

7:     Death with Dignity 77

8:     Fellow Travelers 91

9:     Fairies and Other Beings 113

10:    Relationships 119

11:    Life in Heaven 129

Epilogue 143

About the Author 145

Acknowledgments

While writing this book with Diana, there were times when I stumbled and even questioned myself. I would, therefore, like to thank the following people who never, not even for a moment, doubted that I was communicating with the wonderful spirit of Princess Diana. Their love, encouragement and support got me through my periods of doubt. Each and every one of you knew, even better than I did, that this book would, indeed, become a reality. To one and all, I say "Thank you" from the bottom of my heart: Judy Guggenheim, Lucy Zona, Kaye Champion, Vicki Gioscio, Wendy Beresheim, Tina Michelle and Sylvia Pittman. If I have left anyone out, it is purely an oversight on my part, and please know that I appreciate each and every person who added so much to my life while I wrote this book.

I would also like to thank Tony Stubbs my agent and editor. Tony, I honor and acknowledge you for all of your hard work, dedication and support throughout this long process. You truly are a fine soul!

Claudia Armata, my female knight in shining armor, you have my undying gratitude always, and I also thank Steve Oliverio for his support.

I thank my three sons and my husband for causing me to examine and re-examine my intentions, my heart and my soul on a daily basis while I wrote this book. Because of you, I have found my answers.

Lastly, my deepest and most profound thanks go to Princess Diana herself. Thank you, Diana, for coming into my life and for bestowing on me the honor of carrying your message forth. It is with great love and admiration for you that I do so.

Dedication

My darling boys, I hear your cries; "Mummy, how will we get on without you?"

Your hearts will continue to carry my love for each one of you through your grief. This love will sustain and uplift you both. Try to remember all of our chats regarding my eventual death. No, you did not want to hear me at those times, but I know your souls took in what I was so desperately trying to say. I understand deeply that you feel a constant loss and that one can never be fully prepared in their hearts and souls for the death of their beloved mummy. Please know that I hold you both close to my heart night and day. I watch you always. You are both the best and proudest achievements of my life. Everything else loses its color and its meaning compared to the both of you. There was never anything more important or dear to me during my life other than to be your mummy.

I love you now as I loved you then. Remember, love never dies. I do miss you both terribly even though I am always near. I miss grabbing you up for your hugs. I miss you hugging me back with all your might. If I could, I would return to you both this instant. My boys, know that when we see one another again, we will run into one another's arms and never let go. I promise.

Love to you both forever,
your devoted mummy.

Introduction

Saturday evening, August 30, 1997

"Hey, Mom, Lady Diana's been in an accident. It's on the TV news. It happened in Paris," my 15-year-old son called from the living room. As I shot from the kitchen to the living room, I heard the reporter saying that Diana was unconscious, having sustained a concussion, a broken arm and a severe gash to her thigh. Without saying anything, I walked back into the kitchen in shock, knowing that Princess Diana was gone, that she was with us no longer. Sometimes being psychic is a mixed blessing.

I didn't tell my family that I knew Diana had already passed away. As they continued to watch the news reports, I kept myself busy in the kitchen and hoped and prayed that I'd picked up the wrong information. As I tried to tune out my tumbling thoughts and feelings plus the sounds of the TV set in the next room, I suddenly noticed a stranger standing in my kitchen. Diana!

I shook my head. The news had rattled me and I was obviously imagining things. When I reopened my eyes, Diana had disappeared but suddenly the bottle of soda I'd just taken out of the fridge was knocked out of my hands. It landed squarely on the top of my left foot, fell over with a thump and exploded all over the kitchen floor with a tremendous crash.

"What happened?" my husband shouted, rushing into the kitchen as I limped over to a chair and held my aching, swollen foot. I was speechless and couldn't tell him what had happened. As he cleaned up the mess, I silently asked, *"Who did that and why?"*

Diana was no longer visible in my kitchen but appeared in my mind's eye instead and said, "I'm sorry, but I just wanted to get your attention."

"Well, it worked," I mumbled. "But why?" I asked, hobbling into the living room to watch the rest of the news reports. Later in the evening, the dreadful truth emerged: Lady Diana had passed from this world.

All evening, I still felt her presence around me but instead of connecting with her energy, I stubbornly tried to rationalize it away. I'm a housewife and mother living a typical suburban life in South Carolina, and here's a dead English princess and mother of a future king of England trying to communicate with me. Over and over, I asked myself why would she want to do that.

It's not strictly true to say that I'm Ms. Average America. Since I can remember, I've communicated with non-physical beings, especially angels and sometimes those who have recently passed over. The fact that a recent arrival on the other side was trying to get my attention didn't surprise me but what did surprise me was who it was. As I was to find out, however, her identity would end up mattering less than her message.

Briefly, I see those who communicate with me in full "living" color on a kind of movie screen in my mind. They tell me that all they need do is project a thought of themselves into my mind and, apparently, some special circuitry in my brain picks up their projection and displays it on my internal screen. I also get the "sound-track" in my head and can hear them clearly. Sometimes I speak to them out loud or just think a question in my mind, and they answer immediately. This way, I can converse with them effortlessly.

Normally, I would have opened up to such a "visitor" but not this one. *If I claimed to be in contact with Diana, people would think that I'd really lost it*, I rationalized. I tried shutting her out, but I couldn't turn the screen off, and every time I closed my eyes, she would appear. No matter how long or how hard I tried to shut her image out of my mind, she never wavered or grew fainter.

Finally, I sat down, closed my eyes, and in my mind's eye, saw Diana before me, arms folded, head tilted slightly down and to the left. She held her mouth in a determined line and her piercing blue eyes gripped mine in their gaze.

"Look, why are you here? Why are you communicating with me?" I asked.

She stood in her characteristic shy yet determined stance and very softly said, "Because I wish to do so. I think that you are a very spiritual person. Someone with whom I could connect easily because of the similarities of our energies and our feelings about life and people."

"Now wait a minute," I retorted angrily, "you can't compare our feelings about life. You've led a charmed life. You just turn out for social occasions, smile a lot, and shake a lot of hands."

Boy, did that trigger a reaction. She flared up and her eyes blazed. "You couldn't be more wrong. Regardless of what it looked like from the outside, my life has been tragic on the inside. If you would let me speak through you, you would learn much more about me and my life. And I know that you would do a good job of recording my spiritual journey."

"Look, why don't you try communicating with someone else, like someone from England?" She seemed very amused by my lame attempts to wriggle off the hook. When that didn't work, she pleaded with me, "Please help me. I really need your help."

"Why?" I flat out asked her. Her answer floored me.

"Almost everyone I trusted in my life has let me down in one way or another, but I know that you won't, Christine. I know I can trust you."

When that didn't work, she took on her determined stance again. "Look, I'm not going away until you agree to write a book with me. And I know you can do it without letting your ego get in the way."

Well, she was right on that point. When communicating with angels and other beings, I've learned to get my personality out of the way and just let the information come through even though it doesn't always make sense to me. It always makes sense to my clients, and I've come to trust my psychic abilities.

Then she tilted her head in a question, as if to ask, "Well, what are you waiting for?"

I told Diana that I would think about it. I prayed for guidance, asked my guardian angels, and meditated for hours. On every level, the answer was the same: "Go for it." So I did and let Diana know my decision. I went to my computer and immediately started typing to her dictation.

Initially, I kept all this to myself, but after several days, I decided to let my husband know what was going on. His initial reaction was utter disbelief. I found this hard to take because, even on our first meeting, I made no secret of the fact that I received spiritual information from angels and spirit guides.

He explained, "I don't have a problem with what you're doing but more about how the outside world will react to the fact that it's

Diana. You know you're going to have a tough road ahead if you go public with her story because people simply won't believe that it's really her. How are you going to convince people?"

I, too, was concerned about this so I closed my eyes and Diana was waiting. I relayed the question back to her, adding that it was just going to be too hard on me to write her story.

With calm grace, she said, "I do not think there will be any problem with readers knowing that it is indeed me talking. They will recognize my spirit as they read my words."

What else could I do but accept that. My children, however, were convinced that I'd really flipped. They rolled their eyes and said, "Mom, why would Diana contact you?"

"Good question," I replied, turning once more to Diana.

She answered, "Tell your children that our energies are aligned and that I can communicate especially easily with you because of your abilities."

When I relayed her message to them, they just shrugged and said, "Whatever, mom."

Kids don't like anything that makes them stand out from the crowd, but I didn't let their doubt affect my decision. So, having gotten my family's objections off my chest, I committed fully to let this wonderful woman's energy come through.

At the outset, Diana told me, "Now that you have committed to me, I will commit to you, and will come through you only and no one else. However, I must tell you that there will be another psychic who will overhear our conversations and will try to publish a book about me."

Giving that warning no further thought, we began, and as the two of us wrote her story, I found myself really enjoying working with her, each day looking forward to our next session.

After months of listening and typing, the book was done, or so I thought. I sent the manuscript to dozens of publishers. Day by day, the pile of rejections on my desk mounted—a horrendous experience for a new author. Why was no one was interested in publishing what Diana had to say? In our ongoing sessions together, I asked her, over and over, what the problem was but she remained silent on the matter.

Eventually, I retained a literary agent. At the time, I was pleased because I thought that this proved that a third party who had seen the manuscript really believed that it was Diana. Instead, all it proved was my naïveté to the fact that no reputable literary agent ever charges writers up front to represent their work. This agent took my money and did absolutely nothing with the manuscript. I asked Diana why she didn't warn me about him. She replied that I had not asked her. She was right. I hadn't.

After many months of getting nowhere with the agent, I began to write to many authors of spiritual books, including Judy Guggenheim who, with her husband at the time, had co-authored *Hello From Heaven*, a book on communication with the deceased. After reading it, I e-mailed Judy and asked her for information on obtaining representation for a manuscript. I added that I was writing a famous person's account of heaven.

Judy wrote back and offered me many suggestions, none of which panned out. However, we had formed such good rapport that we continued to communicate via e-mail to the point that she invited me to be a guest speaker on her After-Death Communications web site (www.after-death.com). Since that time, Judy and I have jointly worked together at many public functions with both of us giving public lectures and with me doing spiritual readings.

Having had no success with the publishing establishment, I decided to self-publish and Diana immediately took charge. She had Judy hook me up with Tony Stubbs, an Englishman, a prominent metaphysical author himself, and a professional editor living in Southern California.

When Tony first saw the manuscript, he called me to ask why I had "americanized" Diana's words. That question struck a resounding chord with me because while I had been typing Diana's story, she had repeatedly told me not to change any of her words. But being what some might call an arrogant American, I thought I would "help" her out by changing her wording into "American" English.

Tony pointed out that Diana was, after all, English and that, of course, she would use phrases and words that would reflect her culture. While I was on the phone with Tony, Diana appeared in my mind's eye, vigorously nodding her head in agreement with what he was saying. In typical Diana fashion, she led me gently but firmly to the realization that she will say what she needs to say in her own words, with no "assistance" from me. So, with an English princess and an English editor on my case, what choice did I have but to agree. As an interesting aside, that first phone call took place on the first anniversary of Diana's death.

Through me, Diana and Tony exchanged a few comments about the awful English weather and his hometown, which she had once visited. Then the three of us discussed the manuscript and agreed how we would work together.

At one point in the writing process, I was feeling down about our dictation. Diana was so forthcoming about spiritual information, yet was reluctant to give any information for validation purposes, such as names and dates that weren't already in the public eye. She would just repeat, "That's just not important."

"Yes it is, at least on the level we're on," I argued, but she would just shrug.

One day, she finally explained. "As for my reticence to name names and dates, I had the most God awful propensity while alive to forget names, dates and even geographical locations. I had a sort of learning problem with information and that is why my studies did not go well for me. Harry has the same problem I had, but he is getting help from a private motivational tutor to help him around this. I tried to keep my learning problems a secret from everybody for a long, long time, and when word got out that I was somewhat scatterbrained, I laughed it off and made fun of myself saying that I was 'as thick as a post.' Now that I am in spirit, names are even less important to me.

"Of course, I will never forget Dodi's name, for after all, this was the man I had been contemplating marriage with, although I know now that we would never have been allowed to marry if we had both lived. He was, after all, a playboy and he couldn't have kept faithful to me. Yes, you will be asked why more names are not in my book and you can tell the world that Diana's intent for this book is not a 'tell all' about family and friends, but rather about my spiritual experiences.

"You may also say that it is my desire to mention only those with whom I had major spiritual struggles with while alive, no pun intended towards Major Hewitt! By the way, you may mention his name in the manuscript, as it is well documented that I did have an affair with him. He is something of a preening fool and will feel honored that I mentioned him at all.

"Heaven is exciting and still new to me. I am learning constantly, and constantly seeking also. Oh, Tony, before I forget, there are seven levels in heaven and seven steps in each level. Since I am currently upon the third step of level five, I suspect that I will have to go around a few more times yet! One thing is certain, however. The next time I come back, I will live a much more personally successful life than any of my former lives.

"That's all for now, my friends. Take care and keep going. You both know that Spirit won't let you fall. Your loving friend, Diana."

What you are about to read is Diana's truth in her own words about her after-death experiences and the insights she gained about the life she had just lived. As a mother myself, I relate profoundly to her feelings about leaving her two boys behind, and I found her open letter to them deeply touching.

My most sincere wish is that you will accept the validity of the source of this material and embrace the wisdom it conveys. May her words bless and guide you as you travel with her.

— Christine Toomey

Editor's Note

As you read of Diana's experiences, it is important to remember that what one encounters immediately following death is custom-tailored to that person's individual needs. Someone who was traumatized in life and/or death will need more healing, say, than someone who lived a gentle, peaceful life. Also, the guides and counselors who work with a newly-arrived soul must initially couch their teachings in terms of his or her beliefs about the after-life—heaven, hell, God, and so on.

Also, the counseling takes into account the new arrival's understandings from all previous lifetimes, plus what will be needed for future incarnations. Therefore, individual experiences differ greatly.

What you are about to read is one person's unique experiences told through her personal pictures of reality. They are "typical," in the sense that they illustrate the kind of experience a new arrival can expect.

The fact that Diana tends to use the terms "spirit" and "soul" interchangeably caused some initial confusion, but in discussion, we clarified that "soul" is that eternal, immortal spiritual being that transcends all lifetimes and carefully plans each one, whereas "spirit" is that part of the soul that animates a particular lifetime. There is no difference in *quality*, however, but just in perspective. Spirit serves, therefore, to relay its experiences and understandings back to soul for use by other incarnations that the soul may initiate. What left Diana's body at her death (as with anyone) was the spirit which continued to have a dialogue with the soul, even after death.

Finally, please read Diana's account of her spirit's journey with an open mind and heart. Let her words warm and inspire you, as they did while this beautiful being walked among us.

— Tony Stubbs

Chapter 1

Waking Up

I BLINKED MY EYES SEVERAL TIMES. I WAS SEEING A GOLDEN, glowing, pulsating light, and thought that perhaps I was hallucinating. Although barely conscious, the extent of my injuries was such that part of me could still feel intense pain through every nerve of my body.

The soft yellow glow reached out to me, and suddenly I felt totally free from pain. The doctors and nurses would tell you that that it was just not possible for me to feel pain because I was not conscious when I was brought in to hospital. However, I did feel pain until the soft golden light filtered into me. I was so grateful that the pain was gone. The golden light took form—a beautiful woman. It wasn't so much her appearance that surprised me as much as the energy she emanated. She extended her hand to me without uttering a single word and beckoned me to take it.

I am not good at remembering the titles of books but I had read in people's accounts of near-death experiences that they had gone towards a bright light as they departed this world. So, in view of all the books on the topic and shows on the telly, I expected that when

I died, I, too, would see a bright light. Much to my surprise, I did not. But I did see the beautiful being, although initially, I wasn't really sure whether she was a spirit or an angel. After looking at her, I decided that she was a spirit because she didn't have wings. Her energy was pure goodness and love. She looked to me like the pictures of angels I had seen in many different books—a spirit guide, I supposed. She was unbelievably beautiful and serene, and I felt instantly at peace.

I remembered being in a speeding car racing through a Paris tunnel, and feeling terribly frightened. Somehow, I knew that what was about to happen was intended to cause the death of Dodi Fyad, but two other people would also die; Paul and me. At the time, I didn't know why anyone would want us dead, but I knew that all of our lives would shortly be over. In the depths of my fear and panic I shouted out, "God help us!"

In hindsight, I have a much better idea of what happened to me, Dodi, Paul and Trevor on the night of August 31, 1997, and would like to share as much as I can without jeopardizing anyone's safety.

As Paul tried to outrun the paparazzi, Dodi and I at first thought it was nothing more than a game. We were confident that Paul would lose the paparazzi that were trailing us, for we had encountered this many times before. We were quite used to the nuisance of having to outrun the photographers and so at first, we paid no heed to what was happening. But when Paul stopped laughing and started swearing, a chill went through me, and I think Dodi as well. It was then that he and I realized that it wasn't just the paparazzi chasing us. This was no ordinary cat and mouse game. We had long lost the paparazzi and were now being stalked by those who wanted much more than pictures.

Two people on a motorcycle kept coming faster and faster towards us and even overtook us. The motorcycle with the two people upon it, followed closely by a tan-colored car, pulled up short a few feet in front of us and quickly shone a very bright light into our car. Blinded, Paul lost control of the car and skidded all about the tunnel, eventually running head on into a support. Dodi and I were tossed about inside as if we were nothing more than feathers in the wind.

I was in agony and kept going in and out of consciousness. I heard the motorcycle speed off but saw a man in a leather jacket looking in through the right passenger window. Our eyes met. It was then that he put his hand into his jacket pocket but I could not see what he retrieved from it because I was losing consciousness. However, as I was slipping away, I distinctly heard popping sounds. When I came to again, I called out for Dodi but received no reply.

Dodi had intended to propose marriage to me that evening in his apartment, which was where we were going. I had been nervous and agitated the whole evening long because I knew that I would not be able to marry Dodi because by marrying him, I was in grave danger of losing my boys.

I did not want to forgo any future happiness that Dodi and I may have had, but giving up my boys was something I could never do, no matter what the circumstances. The British Crown was very much against me marrying anyone but a fellow Brit, and Dodi and I both knew this. Dodi did not know that I had reservations about marrying him, however, and the last thing I wanted to do was hurt him. So you can see, I was in quite the muddle, wasn't I?

However, it was now apparent that I would not have to worry about hurting Dodi or losing my sons, for I knew that Dodi was dead and that my life hung in the balance. I felt that Dodi's spirit was no longer with me as I writhed in agony. I knew that the man in the leather jacket had made sure that Dodi was no longer of this world.

The paparazzi caught up to us and took pictures of the carnage. Even in the midst of all of this pain and suffering, there was money to be made. What kind of people would do that? Did they know, by looking at any of us, that we were beyond hope? Of course not! One cannot assume that because a body is covered with blood, its heart does not beat still.

While the paparazzi went about their dastardly business, a passerby who had seen our smashed car from the other side of the tunnel came to our aide. I believe he was a doctor, but what could the poor man do, really? He was ill-prepared for what he found.

I knew that it was too late for Dodi, but I was not sure of Paul's condition or of Trevor's. As it happened, Trevor and I were still alive, and we should have been aided immediately. This being the case, I have a few questions remaining for those who crowded the wreck and photographed its blood-covered occupants. Why didn't any of you help? Why did you continue to take pictures of us, even as you heard my moans? Some of you knew that I was alive, so why then did you not cease your blood sport and summon help? Where was your compassion?

Now that I have crossed over into this beautiful realm, I have the answers that I did not have while I clung to life inside that wrecked car. I have forgiven all of those who caused the deaths of not only myself, but of Dodi and Paul.

It is true that there was a conspiracy to end a life. However, the true purpose was to remove Dodi from this earth, but not necessarily me, as well. It's very intricate and I assure you the mastermind behind the plot will not be found out during that person's lifetime. Keep in mind, however, that God brings everything to light and so, too, eventually will the circumstances surrounding the deaths of Dodi and me become apparent.

You may wonder, with good cause, why there was a conspiracy to murder Dodi. Our relationship caused considerable unease for many people. Due to his love for me, he was hated on both sides of the English Channel and the Mediterranean, as well. Why? There are those who do not like change in any way, shape or form. Change is frightening to those in established power and is most unwelcome. Many Egyptians saw me as an intruder and many British saw Dodi as a menace.

I, too, had been murdered along with Dodi because it had been leaked that Dodi was to propose to me that evening. Because many British as well as Egyptian people were opposed to this marriage, it is important not to jump to conclusions as to who was the most motivated to order our deaths. You see, Dodi had been the original target, but once it was known that an announcement of marriage could be forthcoming at any time after the evening of August 31, 1997, measures were stepped up to ensure that that announcement never came.

Suffice it to say that the instigators of this crime were quite satisfied that their money had indeed been well spent. After all, they got three for the price of one, didn't they? However, this is all I can say without putting anyone else at risk.

Although what I am about to say may sound quite mad, it is important for you to listen. While we are alive, we think that the murder of any person seems most abominable, but at a soul level, all has been planned and agreed to. As you read further in this book, I will explain.

As I gazed upon the beautiful golden spirit, I was aware that I was in between two planes—the earthly and the spiritual. It seemed that I had a choice to make.

The effort to stay alive was daunting and extremely tiring. I no longer wanted to fight and struggle for my life through the agonizing pain: I wanted rest and peace. I found out something rather amazing about what goes on when a person is in between life and death—that the mind and the soul are not always in agreement. Although my injuries were severe, my mind was saying, "Stay and fight. I still have so very much to live for—my two boys. I don't want to leave them and yet I don't want to live hooked up to tubes either."

On the one hand, my soul, was telling me, "Let's go now. It's time to go." But on the other hand, my mind would retort, "Let's wait and think about what you're doing before you take this lovely being's hand. If you do, you will, of course, pass over."

My struggle to stay or to go was short in duration, but a struggle nonetheless. An internal war was going on within me. Deep down, however, I knew there really was no option. Because of the injuries, my body could no longer fight even though my mind was telling it to. My life as I knew it was over and I know now that the medical staff also knew it.

Charles had been informed by telephone that I was in very bad shape. He had been advised that I would not live long even hooked up to the machines. He told the doctor to unhook me and to let me go in peace.

The spirit's smile, so kind and gentle, told me that there was no pain or sorrow where she existed. I, too, desperately wanted to go there. I took her hand knowing that I would be leaving my body behind. I left my body before the doctor could unhook me. I had made the decision to go on before any medical personnel made it for me.

My spirit was instantly removed from my body. I was showered with feelings of peace and love. I am afraid that earthly words are inadequate to describe what I experienced, but I will try, nonetheless. Upon taking my guide's hand, I heard a rushing of sound like ocean waves thundering to the shore. The rushing noise was over in a second and was followed by silence, pure delightful silence.

I felt so very light and free. My body became vaporous and floaty. Small balloons of color flew all around me in every direction. Some of these colored balloons came and rested upon my shoulders. I turned to look at them and tried to touch them but as soon as I did, they burst like water balloons. The color from inside each balloon exploded in a mist and swirled all about me. Every color of the rainbow enveloped me. I thought how very pretty it was to be bathed in a rainbow. Actually, I became the rainbow. I was overwhelmed by a happiness and peace unlike anything I had ever known during life. My guide never let go of my hand during this process. I didn't see her while I was going through the rainbow transformation, but I felt her hand still holding my own.

The rainbow slowly unwrapped itself from around me and flew off, its colors still in formation. I was amazed to see that a rainbow had its own energy. I looked to the spirit for an explanation and she introduced herself to me. "I am Ariel, your spirit guide. That is not my earthly name, but rather the name I chose when I crossed over into spirit."

After letting that sink in, Ariel continued, "Diana, in spirit, everything has an energy field and an ebb and flow of rhythm. As you go further along, you will see what I mean. And, you will always be amazed, as I am, at the spectacularness of this world."

She smiled at my awe and said, "The rainbow was a gathering of spirits to welcome you."

I had never been given a welcome quite as beautiful as that before. It felt so good and loving that I could have absolutely burst.

Hand-in-hand, we flew high above the earth and looked down upon it. We went way out past the moon and as I gazed down at the earth, looking so small like a ball of yarn, I couldn't believe that at one time I had thought that the planet of my existence was everything and all. I had not realized that there is so much more to our universe.

Ariel then said, "You are free to go wherever you choose."

I wasn't sure really what she meant by that. I wondered if she were asking where I wanted to spend my spiritual life. My thoughts were jumbled and confused, so I did not answer immediately. She sensed my confusion and added, "You are free to go to any earthly place that you would like to visit again in order to free yourself from any last minute longings. Where on this earth do you want to visit?"

An idea popped into my mind which really baffled me, "Would you take me to St. James Palace?" I asked her. I don't know why I thought of that place but that is exactly what came to mind. Amazing really. I am sure it is well known by now how much I truly loathed the place while I was alive, so why on earth would I want to go there when I was dead?

Ariel and I also went to Kensington Palace and looked down upon the scene. I saw the crowd grow larger and larger as people came to leave tribute to me. I realized why my spirit had led me here immediately after my death. I needed to see and hear first hand how much I truly was loved. A question that had always haunted me was finally being answered. Was I really loved for me, for being who I was? Most definitely yes!

The first thing I noticed were the flowers piled up against the gate. Bushels and bushels of them flowed out onto the pavements and street. I breathed in the heavenly fragrances of the flowers. I felt totally at peace, filled with happiness and love. Never in my wildest dreams did I think that so many people would turn out for me. Truly unbelievable really. The prayers that I heard, the tears that I saw and the heartfelt emotions that I felt for me and for my boys touched my heart and soul deeply.

I saw the grief that my passing had caused. I next visited my family, giving them comfort and strength through my presence. I also went out amongst the people who were gathering together to comfort one another by leaving flowers and offering support and condolences. This all told me how very much I had been loved. Some, sensing my spirit, caught a glimpse of me as I passed through the crowds. Their soul's cry for me found me and recognized my spirit. Those people who were especially sensitive to psychic energy must have thought that perhaps their minds were playing tricks upon them. However, it really was me and not a trick of the mind at all.

All through the wee hours of the night and into the day the people came. Day after day, even after my funeral at Westminster Abbey, people still left messages and flowers. The high point of my funeral, which I attended, of course, was the very high honor that my very dear friend Elton John paid by singing his beautiful Marilyn Monroe song for me. He is quick on his toes for things like that, Elton is. He is the perfect one to have to come up rather quickly with a song for a dead princess. Very well done, Elton, and thank you, darling. I am so glad that you are tuned in spiritually. You know within your soul that I am finally above it all.

I was utterly amazed to see that so many people around the world grieved my passing. I had been aware that people appreciated my works and the fact that I was, at one time, a royal but I hadn't realized how completely I had been taken into your hearts. To those wonderful people, I would like to say, "I am well; I am happy. And I thank you for the outpouring of love I witnessed shortly after I passed over."

It is no coincidence that my dear friend Mother Teresa passed away shortly after I did. She was aware of how people tend to place their idols on a pedestal, so she asked God a long time ago to take another well-known figure shortly before her own death in order to divert attention from her. My death just before her own served as an answer to her prayer. However, she was still mourned and still is mourned by millions of people. There is just no getting around the fact that greatness will be revered. And Mother Teresa was a great lady. She was far greater than I could ever have hoped to have been. We have chatted up here and she reports that she is most extremely happy to be holding the hand of her Lord Jesus Christ. Of course, her spiritual eyes are especially upon India and she guides her people daily with her spirit.

Since I have been in spirit, I have found that many, many people feel they are liked, admired and perhaps even loved only because of what they can give and contribute to others, but they don't feel loved for who they are. And so I say, let other people know, just as surely as you have let me know, that they are loved. When people honestly know they are loved and accepted for who and how they are, the world and the human souls within it will heal. Love is a powerful energy. It reaches into the hearts and souls of every living thing, healing and uplifting as it goes. To all living things, the benefits of love are enormous and quite evident.

I am in a spiritual realm that is teaching me about self-acceptance and healing. Since arriving here, my journey has not always been easy, as I have had to come face-to-face with myself, but I have found it to be totally worth the effort. As I learn and grow, I will ascend the spiritual ladder towards more self-knowledge and illumination. Many people think that death means that the challenges of life are over, but one of the messages of this book is that death is when the challenges really begin. I will talk much about these challenges in this book.

Another message that I wish to get across is that over here, it's so much harder to right the wrongs you created while you were alive. It's so much easier from your side to bury the hatchet and say to someone with whom you have a grudge, "I am sorry for any hurt I caused you, whether intentional or accidental. Let us go forward with no ill will."

Any serious conflicts or grudges that are left unresolved because one or other of the parties dies do not simply "go away." The parties to the dispute will need to pick up the threads in another life. As you will read later, even though Sarah Ferguson and I loved each other dearly, we will need to incarnate together once more to deal with our much-publicized jealousies and petty rivalries. Setting up the circumstances so that two new personalities will be able to rehash their souls' old issues is such a waste of time and energy. Without the conflict in their lives, those two people could do so much good instead.

From where I am, I can witness people, places and events anywhere within the world at any time. I can hear and see people as they go about their daily life. You may have heard it said that there are other dimensions all around the living. That is so. In my dimension, every spirit here sees the earth, moon, and stars and, of course, the other galaxies, as if by looking through a huge doorway. When you cross over, you will see what I mean. It is rather hard to explain because when you haven't experienced something for yourself, it all seems rather unreal to you. But real it is. That being so, I see that there are others who continue where I left off in the causes that meant so very much to me. Those causes are still so very important to the world's well-being and it is vital that they are continually attended to.

While I am on the subject, I want to take a moment to fully explain how it was that I became involved with so many issues and causes. When I first married, I assumed I would help out with a charity or two, but would devote most of my time to my husband and to the making of a home. I had been told before I married that being Princess of Wales meant, among other things, that I would attend Charles' public duties alongside him. I had not been told however, that I would have to share my husband with another woman.

I am very glad that I did not know at the time that Charles had sought Camilla's approval to marry me. I had assumed, of course, that in their meetings, they were discussing me at length, so I went out of my way to hide my agitation concerning the closeness of their relationship before we were married.

The day of my marriage, I knew that Charles' heart was not joined with mine when I saw that Camilla was still very much in the picture by the cufflinks she had sent him. I thought that perhaps I could change his mind by my actions. If I were an especially good wife to him, willing to share in as many of his duties as possible, perhaps that would turn the tide in my favor. But Charles had no intention of letting anyone else into his heart other than Camilla. He married me because of my blood line and because he needed an heir.

After I realized that my marriage was a sham, I still wanted to give it a go. I was never one to give up easily. In fact, I was always rather bull-headed not to mention shy. Because of my shyness, I was not particularly fond of the idea of public appearances and advised my husband of this before and after we were married. He told me that he would help me through it. However, the offered help was never given and I found myself very much on my own. I watched Charles work his way through the crowds, but found him to be too stiff and formal with the people. Ever the trooper, I braved the large crowds of people and tried to keep my fear in check.

I really needn't have worried at all. Very shortly after we married, I found that people liked it very much when I shook their hands and said just a few words to them. I soon learned that these people were actually very kind and quite excited to be near me and Charles. I thought quite naïvely that Charles and I had finally found something that we could do happily together.

As it turned out, however, I was the bigger draw than Charles was. At first, I was embarrassed by the thought of it but, as Charles pulled away from me more and more, I looked to the people for the love and acceptance that I lacked within my personal life. Soon I began to thoroughly enjoy being out amongst them. I knew that when I shook people's hands and held their babies in my arms, the eyes of those I met were shining. I wasn't sure if it was because they were meeting Diana the person or Diana, Princess of Wales. At that moment in my life, however, I didn't care. I greedily accepted the admiration from the crowds because I needed it so desperately.

The press also fed my need of acceptance for a while. After a time, the press became so bothersome that I dodged them whenever I could. This, however, caused them to become ever more intrusive. All I wanted was to have as normal a life as possible.

The love I accepted from the crowds was not enough, however, to fill the emptiness I felt inside. I anguished over the thought that my marriage was over before it had begun. Charles' commitment to Camilla was steadfast. He had not let go of her before our marriage and had no intentions of letting go of her after it, either. I felt angry, alone and terribly hurt. It was as if I were the butt of a horrible joke or an experiment gone terribly wrong.

When Charles told me that he didn't love me, I began to physically hurt my body. I put myself through such trauma that it is a wonder I survived it all. Everything from slashing my wrists to bulimia was a direct result of my trying to get Charles' love and attention. I wanted Charles to see what he was putting me through and to take me into his arms and tell me that he loved me. When that didn't come about, I thought perhaps that someone he knew well would take him aside and spell out for him that his wife was killing herself over him, that all she wanted was her husband where he belonged, next to her. As we all know, that didn't happen either. Many years after I married Charles, I woke up to the fact that I could not get back what I never had.

With the help of psychiatrists and a few friends, I slowly began to see that I was worthy of respectful behavior towards myself. I had tremendous ups and downs during the time that I so desperately tried to love myself back to wellness. I'm afraid I put my children through some rather hard times because of it. A mother who weeps incessantly and confides in her young children that she is not loved or even liked by her husband is hurting her children.

I was so terribly mixed up at that time that I turned to those I could trust. And who better to trust than a small child?

I knew that my son William would not turn me away. He often comforted me when it was I who should have been comforting him. I would hold Harry in my arms and smother my face into his chest and weep. He would put his little chubby arms around my neck and say, "Mummy no cry," all the while giving me wet kisses and doing his best at two years of age to comfort me.

There were times when I didn't want my children around me because I felt unable to give them what they needed from me.

These absences were never for very long because I loved them and did not want to be away from them for more than a couple of days.

I know their souls now and I know soul deep that they have forgiven me and I am so grateful for that. Although their very early years were traumatic in that, for most of them, they had an unstable mother, I truly feel that it has taught them to be compassionate towards those who are suffering in any way. As I have witnessed both alive and in spirit, my boys are very loving and kind. My funeral spoke volumes concerning that. They paid me the very highest honor they could by insisting over the wishes of the court that they be permitted to escort my body through the streets to Westminster Abbey. Their very private anguish was broadcast for all the world to see and yet they rose above their dislike of being public spectacles to ensure that I was with my boys, protected and loved, one last time.

The various causes for which I was known came to my attention during my healing time and I took them on with great flair. My reasons for this are not commendable, however. I wanted to strike back at Charles by showing him that people loved me more than him and Camilla combined. I made sure that there were many photographers around when I visited AIDS victims in hospital and when I visited nursing homes and other institutions. I took a lover because I wanted to feel feminine, loved and wanted by a man. I spent as much time as I could with our children in public and in private. I burned the candle at both ends trying to show Charles up in every way that I could.

The irony of all of this is that my focus switched from me trying to prove something to my husband to total involvement in reaching out to those who were hurting, to those whom I could help by giving them my time and attention. I gladly went to as many places as I could knowing that I was bringing much needed public awareness to many organizations and charities.

From time to time throughout this book, I will mention some of the difficulties I had in relationships within my life. It is not my wish to hurt or malign anyone that I knew while alive; rather, it is my hope that by sharing these various difficulties, I will be helping someone else to rise above their own private anguish.

In many ways, my marriage to Charles was a double-edged sword. I had a loveless marriage and yet it seemed that it was necessary to go through the agony of it all in order to have my two special boys. More and more, I began to ask the question, why couldn't I have had them with a loving husband? I turned to people who had gone through tests of fire. They had all experienced hurt, rejection and loss in great amounts. But in talking with them, I found that something wonderful had always come out of their torment. I began to understand that no one person's life is really any worse or any better than anyone else's and that God gives to all in his time.

As to the larger picture of why Charles and I didn't have a happy and harmonious life together, at the soul level we planned it out exactly how it happened for the following reasons. The challenge that I chose for that lifetime was one of overcoming self-limiting doubts and vulnerability. Charles was the perfect person for me to hook up with to help me learn how to overcome these weaknesses. At the personality level, I really needed his approval and acceptance, yet he could not give me the needed support and self-assurance that I thought he would. Therefore, thanks to this lifetime with Charles, I learned that no one person can give to your spirit what it needs. We must all actively seek what we need through our own self-development and self-empowerment, and not use another as a crutch to lean on. I wanted Charles to do my growing and learning for me and, of course, he could not.

For his part, Charles' soul purpose for his life is to learn how to love openly and honestly. He chose a cold mother and a distant father so that he would have to find love on his own from outside his family. This accounts for his famous "Whatever love means" remark when asked about love. He was attracted to my spirit, yet not to me, because I exemplified all of the qualities that he desired for himself. Those qualities of openness and a genuinely loving nature were a magnet to him and he found himself attracted to me in a way that he could not explain. Again, it is because of what he saw in my spirit.

Charles and I would do well to remember what we learned from one another during our short time together upon the earth. We will encounter one another again, and I know that my anger towards him is resolved so that I will not be put in the same position with him again. I hope for his sake that he clears away any lingering anger or resentment that he may be holding towards me. I am certain that he would not want to be in the position I was in during our next lifetime together.

I know that curiosity abounds about what my last wishes were. Suffice to say they were left within the confines of my family which is where they shall remain. Remember that although I was a public figure, I had a private life. I know that my wishes towards those that meant everything in the world to me will be carried out.

My purpose in writing this book is to share with you the spiritual truths I have learned while I have been here in what I call, for lack of a better word, "heaven." I am learning many things at an accelerated pace. I could never have absorbed this amount of knowledge within three lifetimes upon earth. Yet it is all so simple that I am amazed that while I was alive, I found life as difficult as I did. So many things make sense to me now that didn't before. I have had my heart and soul touched by the guiding love of countless angels who have held my hand through the difficult parts of learning while I have been here.

Open your hearts and minds as you read these words. Your heavenly helpers, spirit guides and angels are all there right next to you helping you to accept and explore what is written within these pages and beyond.

Everything within your life is understood within your soul. Listening to your soul is the beginning of wisdom. Your life will be so much more meaningful and far less painful if you will only heed the call of your soul. No one will know true happiness until they do so. I used to hear so many references to "knowing yourself." I for one did not fully comprehend the enormous importance of that advice until just before I passed from your world.

To get in touch with your soul, sit quietly and reflect upon your life. Ask for the love of your guardian angel or any other heavenly spirit you have made a connection with. When you ask in this way, you allow all of God's heavenly angels and spiritual guides to communicate with you. God's messenger angels then carry your concerns, joys, hopes and wishes to him. The angels of God fight the darker spirits of the world who would rather that you didn't communicate with God. They want you to be ignorant of the enormous power that is yours as beloved children of God.

Jesus said that, when you pray, believe that your prayers will be answered. If you do not believe something yourself, you are, in fact, telling your soul to discount what you just prayed about. How can you expect God to fulfill your desires and wishes for you if you do not see them as important and real within your own being?

Your spirit guides as well as your guardian angels were sent to you at your birth. They are there for you to work with and to draw strength from. Get in touch with them—they have a host of knowledge to share with you.

Everyone is given a job to do while alive. Mine was not only to heighten public awareness of the less fortunate, but also to be who I really was without trying to bend and shape myself into what others thought I should to be. Actually, my hardest task was to be myself. I am not bitter that shortly after I learned to enjoy being who I truly was, I was removed from the earth. Rather, I am grateful for the time I had and will come back someday carrying this knowledge of self-acceptance with me. It will not be necessary for me to repeat my past soul lessons again.

It may surprise some of you to know that I will come back again. All of us are given many, many opportunities to come back and try our hand again at successful earthly living. My next lifetime on earth will be a great adventure for me. However, I will not have to do a repeat performance of this lifetime's lessons since what I have learned is soul deep and therefore unnecessary to repeat.

My own spiritual awakening started a year before I departed from this world. I was unaware of it at the time because it was a slow and gradual process. I had been asking people about their concept of God and trying to understand the concept of faith. Before this spiritual questioning, I never really felt terribly close to God. As a matter of fact, I had felt for many years that God didn't hear my prayers at all. It seemed nothing ever seemed to improve within my life even though I prayed all the time after marrying Charles.

Now that I am in heaven, I see that faith alone can do so much, faith that there is something greater and stronger than you that looks out for you. This is definitely what makes life bearable for people, especially those who seemingly have no hope, those who are crippled with debt, illness and loneliness. Having God—or whatever you care to call this spiritual being—to hold in your heart and mind can ease your entire life and put it in a whole new perspective. I wish I knew then what I know now.

Moments before I physically died, while I still thought with my conscious mind, all of the knowledge and truths that I had been absorbing spiritually for the past year clicked and fell into place, making my passing easier and more fully understood within my soul. The spirit of God gave me this knowledge as he will give it to you at your time also.

Time no longer holds meaning for me. Viewed from the spiritual dimension, days and nights blur together, creating a gorgeous rainbow of colors and sound.

I wanted the time I spent with my guide, Ariel, to go on forever and I honestly thought that it would. Ariel and I went back up above the universe. She wanted to talk to me about what I would be going through in heaven.

"Diana, you will be learning and growing on every level you will be upon."

"Sorry, Ariel, I'm not too familiar with the concept of levels in heaven."

"You will understand as you experience," Ariel replied.

Before we began my spiritual learning, I asked Ariel, "Tell me about your last earthly life and how you became a spirit guide."

"My last lifetime was one in which I, like you, had achieved notoriety."

That remark prompted me to turn to Ariel and really study her for the first time. I had noticed the beauty of her face when I first saw her, but now I was looking for something more, something familiar.

"But, I don't recognize you. I mean that your presence is not familiar," I said, stumbling over my words.

"No, you wouldn't recognize me now because I have a new appearance. The human appearance dissolves and what is left is the look of the soul," she explained.

"Well, why is it, then, that I can still feel my eyes open wide and everything else about my physical body? Doesn't that change, too?"

Ariel patted my hand, which by the way I could feel, and said, "Diana, there is so much for you to learn. Let's just take this one step at a time, so as not to overwhelm you."

I used to think that spirits knew everything once they passed over, but I saw then that I was wrong. Ariel explained, "Spirits in passing over know everything concerning the life they have just led, but not, however, everything about being in spirit."

"Perhaps you're right. One thing at a time," I laughed. "So tell me about your last earthly life."

Ariel resumed, "I, too, was royalty. And like you, I walked a lonely heart path. My people loved me, but I never had the total love of a man. Can you guess who I was in my last lifetime?"

I could guess but was hesitant, so Ariel prodded me humorously, "Go on, take a chance."

"Well," I began tentatively, "my first guess would be Queen Elizabeth the First."

I looked down immediately at my vapory toes after what was probably a most ridiculous guess. I wiggled them to see if I could. I could. Utterly amazing, I thought.

"That's not ridiculous at all, my dear. It so happens that you are correct."

My spiritual guide was Elizabeth the First? Now I knew that I had to be in hospital on some type of mind-altering drug! Ariel laughed as she read that thought going through my mind. "No, Diana, you are not in hospital. And I am no longer Elizabeth the First. Neither of us are who we were while alive. Those were just roles that we played for a short while and then stopped once we were in back in spirit. Do you understand?"

"I understand, but that was a long time ago. Why didn't you come back since then?"

She stood up and extended her hand to me once again, as she did in hospital. "I had so much learning to do, Diana. That lifetime was traumatic for my soul and I had a lot of healing to go through. Once I was finished with that business, I was presented with the opportunity to become a spirit guide. I accepted the healing angels' offer and … well … here I am."

"Have you been a spirit guide to others?" I asked.

"Yes, but I've been your guide every time you've been royalty."

I thought about that as I stood up to take her hand. "How many times have I been royalty, Ariel?"

"In twenty-five lifetimes, Diana."

I started giggling at the thought that I had been related over and over again to myself. "It's rather funny to think that when I studied the royal histories throughout my schooling, I had been reading all along about myself," I laughed to Ariel.

"Different aspects, Diana, just different aspects," Ariel chuckled back.

At school, I had been fascinated by Tudor and Stuart history, particularly the kings and queens and their courts. Needless to say, my fascination stemmed from having lived many lifetimes in that historical period. I was not always a royal in those lifetimes, but I was always connected to the royal families in one way or another, perhaps by being a lady-in-waiting, and once as a stable boy.

A sudden thought occurred to me and I just had to ask. "Ariel, if I had been royal so many times, why did I have such a hard time getting the hang of it during this past lifetime?"

As we once again became airborne, Ariel replied, "We bring to each lifetime those traits that we must work at overcoming. You chose for this last lifetime to be shy and ill at ease with people. The basic knowledge that you needed to have in order to assume your royal role was always there, but you needed to pull it up from your soul in order for it to manifest within your life."

I thought of what my guide had told me while I flew with her to who knew where. I didn't care. All of heaven was so utterly calm and serene that I was sure to fall in love with wherever we landed.

Then in the blink of an eye, it all changed.

Chapter 2

Exile on Pebble Island

I WAS SUDDENLY VERY MUCH ALONE IN A PLACE I DID NOT RECOGNIZE. I spun around looking for Ariel, calling out her name. For the first time since I had crossed over, I felt something other than total joy. I felt more than a little scared. Frantic would sum it up rather well, actually. What I didn't know at the time was that I had been put in a place where I was to learn spiritual truths alone and undistracted.

I found myself in a barren area where there was no sound, no breeze and nothing to look at except for a few pebbles strewn about on the ground. It looked very much like a country road. Looking up, I saw a blue sky. Looking to the left and to the right of me I saw endless stretches of road with no trees, bushes, flowers or plants. I named the lonely place Pebble Island.

I didn't know where I was but I knew I didn't like it. I began to question whether or not I had actually crossed over. Perhaps I would wake up in hospital at any moment.

Ariel appeared in my mind's eye to settle my thoughts and get me moving in the right direction. She told me that I was sent there, separated from everyone and everything, in order to learn how to be okay with the idea of being alone.

"Wait, Ariel, don't go, don't leave me here all alone!" I cried out for Ariel to appear again by my side.

"Diana, calm yourself. You are not alone. This time has been given to you for your soul to speak its truth to you. Please listen to it, for it is a wise teacher."

I threw myself onto the pebbly ground. I suddenly realized once again that I could physically feel things. "Ariel, please tell me why I can still feel with my body?"

"Just because something is not visible does not mean that it does not exist."

"What do I look like exactly?" I couldn't help myself from inquiring, looks had become such a mainstay during my adult years upon the earth.

Ariel replied, "Appearances are not important, Diana. However, it is important for you to know that spirits can feel, taste and smell things more so now than when in human form. Heaven is a place of unlimited beauty which must be experienced with all of the senses to fully comprehend what a true paradise it is."

I then strolled about to consider all that Ariel and I had discussed. I found it all too confusing, so I began to think of other things. I was absentmindedly kicking pebbles with the tip of my toe when it occurred to me that I had been searching my whole life for someone to keep me from feeling all alone. I wondered if I had felt the same in all of my other lifetimes, as well. I believed in reincarnation during my lifetime and still believed it to be true even as I was "in spirit," as Ariel called it.

The events of my most recent lifetime were still fresh within my mind. I decided right then and there to learn and retain anything and everything Ariel put before me. I did not want to go through another lifetime of uncertainty and doubt about myself and my relationships. I wanted desperately to learn how to be strong and independent, to learn to stand on my own with confidence, without needing another to bolster me up. I wanted to keep my sensitivity and kindness, knowing one of my greatest and most important assets was my ability to reach others.

I sat amongst the pebbles, scooping them up then letting them fall just because it was amazing to do so without seeing my arm and hand actually in front of me making this so.

I didn't care for the stillness of the place and wanted to hear music. While alive, total silence had always bothered me. I found I was no different in death. Aching to have someone next to me to chat with or even to be with, I angrily pushed myself up from the ground and ran screaming and crying down the lane. I suppose I had a real hissy fit but it did me good. It cleared the ache out of my system and then I was able to concentrate on the matters at hand.

I dug my toes into the soft dirt and objectively watched myself reacting to specific moments and events. It then occurred to me that if I had believed in myself as a whole and competent person, I could have avoided so much self-inflicted misery. I saw where my lack of confidence had caused me to make some really terrible decisions. It is important for me to expand on some of the poor decisions I had made while alive for, you see, I am requesting forgiveness from the people that I hurt the most.

To all of my chums and flat-mates that I had before becoming a royal, I say I'm so terribly sorry for letting our friendship go. Once the engagement was announced, the Royal Court insisted that I did so, but even so, I should have listened to my heart and not to the court. I did as I was told because I did not want to incur royal disfavor so early on. All of you are ever on my mind and I do watch for you to keep you safe as you go about your lives.

Please understand also that it was far easier for me to maintain friendships I had made after becoming a royal because these people moved within the same circles as I and could jet about with me with no restraints upon them. I do not want to come off as snobby or above it all, but I want you to understand that even if I had tried to continue being your friend, it could never have been like it was before I married Charles. Simply know in your hearts, however, that I treasured every one of you and still do.

James Hewitt was another bad mistake in that by being with him, I was running from the realities of my life and not facing them. James permitted me to believe that we could have a fantastic life together even though I was married to Charles. He kept the fantasy alive within my mind for far too long. When James realized that his involvement with me was making me rather unstable, he ended our affair. However, that ending nearly cost me my mind. I was not yet ready to be without a man to lean upon and he knew that. Seeing all of this from my current vantage point, I now realize that James had become frightened. His position was precarious indeed. After all, he was employed by my husband, an irony we found quite funny, actually.

I let myself be swept away in my fantasy of James Hewitt. You see, I had mistakenly thought that I was in love with him. The truth of the matter is that he showed me tenderness and patience while instructing me in horsemanship and I mistook that for love. Also, Charles was spending as much time as he could with Camilla and telling me that he really couldn't give a fig about my feelings. Well, I for one was going to show him, future king or not!

I gave James signals that I was interested in having a relationship with him. Poor James, he was in for the time of his life. However, I truly believe he enjoyed our time together. By the way, it was not a purely sexual relationship for there were many times James and I discussed deep and far reaching things as well as the silly little things in life. He could dissolve me into fits of laughter like no other. I felt connected to his kindness and want him to know that. I also want him to be aware that he made me realize my potential as a woman. Thank you, James, for suffering through one of the most horrendous times of my life right alongside me. I do believe you both saved and changed my life. We are friends forever.

I used to think for a long time that marrying Charles was the worst thing I could have ever done. Many years before I passed, however, I realized that if I had not, I would not have had my two darling boys. My marriage was awful and filled with sadness, however, my boys kept me alive. Of that, I have no doubt. They brought laughter into my life and the enormity of their love was like a balm to my aching heart.

When I found my life unraveling shortly after I married, I turned to people I had assumed would give me their full support and guidance. As it turned out, my assumption was in error. One person in particular, about whom I had always thought the world, said, "Oh for Christ's sake, Diana, buck up, won't you? Men are always jumping in and out of ladies' beds. That's just the way it is, dovey. You can't change things now anyway, can you?"

What my family and friends failed to understand was the enormity of my unhappiness and that Charles' infidelity was an overwhelming source of great unhappiness. But that was not the only thing causing me unhappiness—with no one to turn to, I felt alone, scared and unsure of what to do.

From the depths of my despair, I had called out to God but
hadn't heard his answer and assumed that he, too, had abandoned
me. I did not know to seek his answer within the quietness of my
soul. All I knew to do was to fill up my every waking moment with
things to do, places to go and people to see. I made sure that there
was hardly any time at all when I was alone. I felt adrift and helpless
when alone, therefore, I filled my calendar up with lots and lots of
events.

I wanted God to wave his magic wand and make everything
right again instantly. When that didn't happen, I became frustrated
and bitter and decided to take matters into my own hands. I began
to do things that some people have said were psychotic forms of
behavior. I have to admit, they were. For example, the bulimia that
I thought I could control physically hurt me almost beyond repair.
The love affairs that I entered into with hopes of finding true love
and acceptance all ended disastrously.

My self esteem plummeted lower and lower each time I did
something that hurt me physically and emotionally but I could not
stop my self-punishment. I knew that I was on a reckless course
and that, without help, would continue to grow and escalate in an
alarmingly dangerous way. Everything in my life was out of control,
even me.

One particularly distressing situation had to do with Oliver
Hoare. He appealed to me because I liked his looks and his manner.
I thought an affair with him would be just a fun diversion for me
because, at the time I met him, I was not seeing anyone and was
lonely. I had become quite callous by the time I met him and didn't
care that he was married. He broke off the affair and this angered
me. I called him at his home several times and caused a lot of strain
for him and his marriage. I just couldn't believe that an art dealer
would dump me and choose his wife over me. It was a very painful
time for my ego since it took quite a bruising from Oliver's decision
to end the relationship. Although I knew he was not the great love
of my life, I was not ready for the relationship to end when it did.
Hence the constant phone calls and my grasping, border-line
psychotic behavior, reminiscent of many years earlier with Charles
when he too pulled away from me.

Why couldn't I find someone to love me as much as the public
loved me? I constantly asked myself and began to think that perhaps
I would be better off dead.

It wasn't until I had endured many years of suffering that I met a trusted advisor and friend who helped me to uncover my deeply buried soul knowledge. She was someone familiar with the royal family and yet, of her own accord, stayed distant from them. I had known of her for years and yet was told to avoid her as she wasn't "one of us." She had royal ties, though, and was told to attend functions when it was necessary for her to make an appearance. I had kept my distance from her as I didn't want to incur the wrath of the court, yet I wanted to know this person who was very independent and stayed aloof from the rest of us. I called her the day I decided to stop playing the role of victim. That was also the time Charles and I had decided to separate but before it had been announced publicly.[1]

My confidante invited me for tea and from there we became fast friends. This wonderful woman helped me to get in touch with my soul simply by teaching me to listen to it through meditation. She also told me of the healing benefits of yoga and encouraged me to practice it, which I did off and on for the remainder of my life. It was difficult for me to get totally involved with yoga, though, because I preferred more active therapy—I like to do rather than sit.

Once I got in touch with my soul, thanks to the advice and wisdom of my dear friend, life improved dramatically. I was told by my soul that before I could move forward with my life, I would have to forgive myself and love myself as I was. Accepting these truths set me on my feet once again and I began to heal.

While on Pebble Island, I reviewed, accepted and learned that I had been the first to let myself down. I had let others define who I was and had sought validation from everyone I encountered. I never wanted to be alone because then I would feel adrift and without guidance. I had wanted people around me constantly to support and lead me.

As I reviewed the why's of my past life, I realized that I had been looking outside of myself for the answers that only my inner self would know. As soon as that truth hit me, Ariel appeared next to me and asked, "Well, do you think you are ready to go on to the next level?"

"Yes, I think so. And thank you for bringing me here. I've learned a lot here but I hope I won't ever have to return."

The lonely, barren pebble-strewn place I was leaving had been perfect for me to come to terms with my discomfort at being alone. Taking hold of Ariel's hand, we left Pebble Island—the place of solitude—and I looked forward eagerly to my next great learning adventure.

As Ariel and I flew, she explained, "While you are in spirit, you pick and choose which traits you will wrestle with and try to overcome within your lifetime. It is all for the sake of your soul's growth. Some traits you are proud of and allow yourself to build upon, such as artistic ability, athletic ability or communication skills. Other traits you are not so proud of and you either run from them or flaunt them with a devil-may-care attitude. The truth is, however, you must work on overcoming what you view as negative traits, such as insecurity and shyness, in order for you to be able to fulfill the reasons why you incarnated in the first place and achieve what your soul intended."

I want the lessons I learned there to be nestled within my soul forever because I do not wish to ever be on Pebble Island again. I saw clearly now that the lessons I had set up for myself in my lifetime were to learn to be okay with the thought of me, to not look for anything or anyone else to complete me and to know that I am complete in and of myself. I also learned that it is pointless to compete with anyone else. I am no better or no worse than someone who is more talented, charming or pretty than I am.

Knowing that, I cannot expect myself to be everything and all to every person. I also saw that I had tried so very hard to manipulate myself into being what my husband and his family thought I should be. I complied, badly I might add, in order to win their favor and approval. If I had accepted myself first and foremost, than it wouldn't have mattered what anyone, including the royals, thought of me.

The hardest lesson to learn during my lifetime and probably yours as well, is to love yourself and accept yourself as you are at this moment. If I would have done that sooner rather than later in my life, I would have been a much happier person. If you do not do this, you, too, will be tossed about like a leaf in the wind. Decide that you and you alone are all you'll ever need, and that anyone else in your life whom you think of as a blessing is frosting on the cake.

This newfound knowledge filled me with a strength and strong desire to pass this information on. When Ariel sensed this, she asked, "Do you think that you are ready to connect with a living person who can pick up on your energy and put your thoughts into words?"

"What? You mean write a book? Yes, I'm game for that and would love to do it."

Like all spirits, I can feel energy from the people upon the earth and my senses scanned the earth looking for the energy field that I felt most comfortable with. At last, I found such an energy, and on the night of my passing from the earth, August 31, 1997, I connected with Christine Toomey's spirit.

You might wonder how this is possible. How could I have gone through all these experiences and still contact Christine within hours of my death? The answer is simple. The concept and experience of time is so very different on this side. I can go to any point in time simply by thinking of it. And all my conversations with Ariel and my visit to Pebble Island occurred in just a few seconds of earth time.

I saw Christine in her kitchen and knew that she could see me very clearly within her mind's eye, but she couldn't believe that it was I who was coming to her. She tried ignoring me, but when that didn't work, she finally sat down and asked, "Look, why are you here?"

I told her, "I find you to be a very spiritual person, one with whom I can connect easily because of it. And I have the utmost confidence in your abilities to write my spiritual account."

Then I told her, "Your spiritual energy and mine are very similar. We share similar feelings about life and people."

Needless to say, this caused all sorts of protests from Christine. She had thought my main objective in life was to please everyone and to smile while doing it. She was wrong. I corrected her thinking and set her straight on that.

"I can think of a million reasons why you should connect with someone else," she said. "Perhaps you'd be more comfortable communicating with someone from England."

That was my favorite and I replied, "Perhaps it's your own comfort and not mine that you are concerned about."

Her logical, analytical side argued with me for quite a while and at one point I said, "Christine, I really need your help."

"Why?" she asked, pointedly.

"Just about everyone I trusted in my life let me down and I need to learn to trust again. I know in my soul that you won't let me down. You have a high degree of spirituality within your soul, and I know beyond a doubt that you will write what I want you to without putting your own ego or influence into it."

She was still not convinced, so I told her, "Look, you and I both know that there already many, many books written about my life while I lived and that there will be many more. But how many will continue the story of *my* life? My *spiritual* life? People will think that my life is over now and that is simply not true. Yes, my earthly life may be over but my spiritual life has just begun and I can still make a difference in people's lives."

Puzzled, Christine asked, "How can you make a difference now, Diana. You're gone."

"Don't you see?" I replied, "When people read and understand that I still feel strongly about all the things that I cared about while alive, it will motivate them to continue my efforts. Also, keep in mind that I am going to talk to people about my spiritual learning so that if they apply what I've learned while they are still alive, their lives will be so much the better for them and, in effect, for the universe as well. Listen, Christine, it is important that this book be written not for my glorification, but so that I can continue to teach and to heal people. A spiritual truth says that when one person is taught, then eventually so are others." Then I added, "Besides, I'm not going away until this book is written."

After a lot of prayer, soul-searching and meditation, Christine agreed to let my thoughts come through and she started typing.

Since starting this book with Christine, I have continued through many levels of learning. I am alone, but not lonely. I am being prepared for unity with other spirits who encountered the same life lessons I did. Once we have obtained full spiritual knowledge, we will then jointly work towards creating greater earthly awareness of spiritual truths and concepts.

Reading this, it would appear that I learned and experienced everything spiritually overnight. In earth time, that would be correct. But as I said earlier, on the spiritual plane, there is no time measurement. A spiritual being receives guidance and learning at a pace unknown to the human experience.

The world's people need spiritual learning so desperately. Without it, violence, hatred, prejudice, negativity and all the ills that plague humanity will continue to thrive. The toll upon the earth and its people will continue to be very high indeed. This is why it is imperative that I share these insights with all of you. We need to start healing our world.

People who have lived and passed over into spirit many times over are being reborn with greater spiritual knowledge each time they reincarnate. They hold positions such as teachers, writers, religious leaders, psychics and policy makers. As with any human being, they are not exempt from experiencing pain, fear or sadness. Rather, because of their spiritual callings, they more often than not have harsher life experiences than most do. Yet, they rise above it all and impart their soul's knowledge to increase spiritual awareness for the sake of all humanity. Highly evolved souls have the spiritual strength to overcome and transform negativity within their personal lives because they have learned and retained many spiritual truths. If you take their teachings to heart, your life will be filled with more joy and happiness and less pain. Their teachings will open you to the knowledge within your own soul and you will discover the many wonderful truths that you have hidden there.

A simple way to begin to access your soul's knowledge is for you to really listen the next time you attend church, talk with a trusted advisor or sit quietly to listen to your own thoughts. Pay close attention to how you feel about what is being said. Take the information into your very being. Your soul will let you know by your level of comfort or as the case may be, discomfort, if it bears truth to you or not.

If it does not sound right to you, ask yourself internally why it does not. Wait on the answer. Do not be in a rush to understand what is foreign or difficult at first. Mull thoughts and concepts over within your mind. Hold them up to past experiences, past advice and past conditioning. You very well may be uncomfortable with information that is actually much needed for your spiritual growth. It's all right if you feel uncomfortable about spiritual truths at first. Just remember that growth is never easy and is often resisted when it is first encountered.

As you start to see and hear spirituality in action, the light of these truths will shine in the darkened regions of your mind. Your spirit will be released from its sparse existence and will come fully alive, enabling you to accept and permit untold blessings and fulfillment to overflow into your life.

Every person and thing within your present life was agreed to by God, your soul and your spirit guide while you were in spirit. All of the experiences you have had in your lifetime were designed to help you learn and grow spiritually. This may be hard to accept at first because many of you cannot fathom that you would have chosen the lives you now lead. But choose you did.

When you are on the spiritual plane, you learn from your guides and spiritual leaders what truths you must possess within your soul while in human form. If you surmount earthly difficulties without losing sight of your soul's knowledge, you progress upon the spiritual plane when you return to spirit.

Some of you do not believe in the existence of heaven. However, it is the truth of the place that I inhabit at this time. It is the place every soul yearns to dwell in forever, but cannot do so until it has reached completion, completion being a soul's experience of every condition known to humanity. The soul will have lifetimes of wealth, poverty, beauty, homeliness, being loved and unloved. After that, a soul is free of any further struggle. It has lived many times and knows the true value of itself. The culmination of all its earthly lives leads up to the realization that it is eternal and greatly loved by its creator.

People may nod their heads and agree that a soul is eternal. The question is; what is eternity? The human mind cannot conceive of, let alone grasp, the enormity of this question, and I regret that I am unable to even begin to explain the concept to you.

Earlier I said that angels fight to get our prayers and desires to God. God, who is perfect cannot allow us to enter into his presence until we have made ourselves perfect through our many lifetimes. Angels, God's messengers, enter into his presence on our behalf. However, before they can get there, they have to literally fight their way to him.

On the other hand, there are all sorts of negative spirits wandering the earth. Most are spirits that refuse to go to the spiritual plane. They want to stop the angels from their appointed duties in administering to the soul's needs. They want desperately to make people's lives as miserable as theirs had been while they were alive. This does not include spirits who, like me, come back for a time to communicate with or help those who are still alive upon the earth.

As there is a heaven, there is also a sort of hell. Again, I say this as one who has been filled with the knowledge of this spiritual place that I now inhabit. That being so, I have learned that hell, or the spirit's perception of it, is a place where the spirit feels totally separate from God. Once a spirit enters into this place, fully and of its own accord, it goes through a period of thinking that it can never leave.[2]

Once the spirit thinks that it has doomed itself to eternal suffering and misery by seeing its past life mistakes and tragedies played out over and over again, it is then free to feel the remorse that it did not while alive. By feeling remorse, it is in effect saying that it is sorry for whatever wrongdoing it had done against humanity. Then ministering angels come to the spirit and help it to heal and forgive itself. Once that is accomplished, the spirit is then made aware that it had never lost its eternal connection to God and is then allowed to proceed with its own unique spiritual learning and growth. All souls have full knowledge of this truth when they are created but, as humans, we sometimes get off track and lose our way.

At the time of death, depending upon the soul's leading, the spirit will know where it is headed—whether to my type of heaven or perhaps the spirit's own personal idea of hell. Going to that sort of hell is really self-imposed and quite unnecessary. The spirit that thinks it can perpetrate any sort of outrage against humanity and get away with it, so to speak, will not be honored by God until that spirit has seen the error of its ways. However, some spirits are extremely arrogant and insist that they would never be turned away by God. Understand that God cannot allow spirits into heaven who have broken the basic spiritual laws which are as follows: Love and serve one another always. Treat one another kindly and forgive one another your mistakes.

To those who are in power, I beg you not to use your God-given power in any way other than for the advancement and protection of your people.

God will treat rebellious and hard-hearted spirits as children in need of discipline. He welcomes back only those who have upheld his spiritual laws within their hearts and minds and by their actions.

God has allowed the image of hell to exist within non-spiritual minds not because he wants to frighten them into believing in him but rather because he wants those who reject him to experience time without him.

Do you demand that your family and friends visit you, or do you give them that choice freely with no strings attached? Like God, you would not want those you love and care about to be with you out of a sense of duty or obligation, but rather with a sincere desire from the heart.

Clearly, these are my understandings and I do not profess to be a theologian. My statements are based upon what I have learned while in this realm. Perhaps your lessons in spirit will differ from my own.

---

[1] Diana and Charles decided to separate early in December, 1992. The Prime Minister formally announced the separation to the House of Commons on December 9, 1992.

[2] Initially, Diana had said that once a soul goes to hell, it is doomed to reside there eternally. When Tony, my editor, questioned her on this, Diana relayed a lengthy message for him through me. This message is included in its entirety since it reveals the process of clarification that often had to take place.

"Christine, tell Tony that he is correct in that if a soul THINKS it is doomed to be separated from God, then it will be, at least for a time. Spirit truth is vastly different from human truth. That is, those who have fear of God while alive will experience a fearful God while in spirit. To fear God is to shun God. God is not an actual being, but an all-compassing spirit. It is extremely hard to describe God, even from my spiritual vantage point. Christians say that to fear God is the beginning of wisdom. I say replace the word 'fear' with 'love.' So, to love God is the beginning of true wisdom.

"When a soul loves God, it loves itself, thereby continuing the spiritual flow, rather like a continuous circle. Do you know what I mean? I never intended to convey that souls are doomed, rather their own thinking while alive is a sort of road map that their soul reads and then goes to when they depart your world. That is why I said that if a soul does not want to be with God, it simply isn't. I am not sure of the length of time and perhaps I should change the passage where I stated that a soul is separate for ever. Sorry, I must have tripped my meaning up somehow.

"Communicating is difficult for two reasons. Firstly, although Christine and I use the same basic English, I use the Queen's English, which is quite proper. Secondly, spirits such as I use certain terms loosely and humans latch onto those terms as if they were written in stone. Sorry, Christine, I don't mean to insult, rather I am trying to explain how it is that you and I sometimes have what some would say is a breakdown in communications.

"Tony, you are a wise and good friend of mine and I know absolutely that you will guide this manuscript to perfection. You will know what I am saying more than Christine does. Again, no slight intended to Christine. I was often scolded for my use of words while alive and I find that, while in spirit, I still have the nagging problem of word usage. Peace to you both and know that you are ever guided by a thousand loving, unseen hands."

Chapter 3

The Level of Healing

A S WE FLOATED TOWARDS THE NEXT LEVEL, I HEARD BEAUTIFUL soothing music coming from instruments I had never heard before. Angels, pastel colors, music and gentle voices were all about me. It was as if I had stepped inside of an angel painting by a great master. It was glorious and wonderful, more peaceful and serene than anything I had ever known before. As angels flew around and about, the swishing of their garments created a perfumed breeze that filled me with an unknown longing deep within my soul.

Ariel took me to a room lit softly, as if by candle glow. She led me to a fluffy bed in the middle of the room. I hadn't realized how tired I was and it seemed as if I were asleep before I lay upon the bed.

I began to dream immediately. One of the angels I had seen earlier hovered over me. Her face was sweet and loving as was her sing-song voice. She said that during my time on earth I had helped and healed many people. For allowing the spirit of healing to work through me, the healing angels invited me to stay with them. I would not have to go onto any other levels of learning if I chose to stay. However, I was not to be an angel, which no human can ever become, but a guide upon this spiritual level.

When I started my public works throughout the world, I was not aware at the time that I was heeding the call of angels. Rather, I'd assumed that I was merely responding to the written requests presented to me by various organizations. These organizations sought my assistance in creating public awareness for their charities by way of my attendance at their fund raisers and by going to hospital to personally visit with people stricken with various maladies.

The AIDS cause touched my heart deeply because of its intrusion upon the lives of my personal friends and associates by claiming the lives of their loved ones.[1] Whatever I did to help that very worthy organization was not anywhere near what it did for me. It touched my heart and soul profoundly when I sat and held the hand of a person who had been shunned because of the disease. To see within their eyes the deep sorrow and longing for acceptance and love was so horribly sad to me. How could anyone turn away from these very special people?

The people I visited in hospital who had contracted AIDS were so very grateful to have a hand to hold onto, if even for a moment. Someone to touch their hand was all that they asked for. How could I not? I found that my ignorance had kept me from helping those who needed it the most. I vowed after seeing the victims of AIDS that I would never again allow ignorance to get in the way of my helping to bring public attention to the worthwhile causes of the world.

Another of those causes was the landmine issue. Representatives from that cause contacted me and asked for my assistance in bringing this issue to the public eye. I went to Bosnia at their invitation to see for myself the destruction that these landmines caused. I was not prepared for what I saw.

I had, of course, been told many times over about the loss of limbs and lives that these people had endured. However, seeing for oneself brings the reality home. It was ghastly and a total waste: countless people, both young and old, who had lost not only parts of their bodies, but loved ones and homes as well. They coped with it all rather well, actually. Much better than I did. The people I met who had suffered a loss because of the landmines had a sad acceptance of their fate.

After public attention had been brought to this issue, donations and aid poured in from around the world. Those who had lost arms and legs received prosthetics that enabled them to walk and to hold onto the outstretched hands of their loved ones once again. They are beginning the slow and gradual process of healing within their hearts and minds.

Their courage and fortitude made me all the more outraged that the landmines, although no longer needed, were still there. I fought tirelessly to have each and every landmine detonated and removed. I know that I stepped on a few international toes with my campaign and angered quite a few people who felt that I was sticking my nose where it didn't belong. However, we all live in this world together and what effects one will, in time, affect us all. We can each make a difference and we should, especially those of you who are in the public eye. Please be a voice for those who have none. I am quite glad to see that the war against landmines is still being fought. In time, we will win this war.

The angel told me, "At any time, you could have turned aside from the urging to help others. However, with your own free will in action, you were a willing soul for the healing angels to work through."

It is the same within your own life, as well. If you feel a gentle urging or leading to do something that may be slightly out of your comfort level, it may be that you are in the presence of an angel asking you to be used for someone else's spiritual growth and gain, as well as for your own.

The angel explained to me, "We live only to serve God and to do his will in a perpetual state of grace. As his messengers, we come to earth to minister to the human souls upon it. Once our missions are completed, we return to the sanctity of our heavenly realm."

It was most tempting to stay forever protected and nourished with the precious angelic spirits that had been enfolding me within their care, yet my desire to learn and grow spiritually was leading me onward. Ariel touched my forehead lightly with her hand and I awoke.

The angels were still flying about and playing music as Ariel and I departed from this healing level. As we left, Ariel told me, "The healing angels educate newcomers on their spiritual plane through dreams. The newly-arrived souls accept and grasp concepts calmly and completely while in the soothing aura of the dream state."

Then Ariel asked, "What did you learn while you were on that level?"

I explained, "I now understand that everyone on the earth gives or denies permission to be used by a spiritual presence, both consciously and subconsciously."

I urge you to open up to the spiritual guidance in your lives. Believe that angels and your guides can and do work through you. Remember that you are never alone, even in your darkest hours. When you don't hear or feel guidance, nothing is wrong so do not be alarmed. There are times when your soul knows to be quiet in order for your mind to absorb and contemplate new information. The human mind needs time to analyze information as it takes it in. You would grow weary of your soul speaking to you continually, telling you all that it knows. It will proclaim and reassert itself within you when you are once again ready to go on in your growth towards greater knowledge of spiritual truths.

I asked Ariel, "Why have I not seen any other human souls upon the levels I have been on thus far?"

She told me, "Heaven is filled with millions of human souls who are on various levels of learning. You have not yet been put in their midst because you still need individual learning and healing. The time will come when you will be with souls known and unknown to you during the time you have lived. At that point, you would all be on the same level of understanding."

My memory had not dissolved upon my death. I remembered relatives and friends who had passed on before me, and very eagerly anticipated being reunited with them. It made me even more determined to get to the next level and absorb every scrap of knowledge it contained.

As we flew, I turned my eyes to my family upon the earth. In earth time, this would have been only days after I passed. Most of my family were in London, but a few were not yet there. I went to one and all no matter where they were at the time. I visited each one individually. They were sorely grieving for me, and I went with Ariel to comfort them. Some of them sensed my presence and were comforted by it. Those who did not feel me near them were still too filled with grief and had closed their hearts and minds to blot out their pain.

I lightly touched the tops of my loved one's heads, leaving them with a blessing of comfort, love and joy before going back to my heavenly home. I told each one of them that a part of my spirit will always be with them. This is true of any spirit. The loss of a loved one does not mean that they are far away and cannot see or be near you. It is quite all right to call upon the name of your departed loved ones to honor and bless them as they travel upon their own spiritual journeys.

My family, like everyone else, have spirit guides. As my family learns to listen to their guides, they will be reminded that I am near. There is no anguish or sorrow within me because I know that someday we will be reunited again, which in spiritual terms is not long at all.

When you have crossed over to the spiritual realm, you can leave parts of your spirit wherever you choose. My family will have the part of me needed to help them come to terms with the loss of my physical presence within their lives. Their guides are telling them to be kind and patient with themselves, because healing takes time. Do not grieve for those who have departed. Their lives are so much better, richer and fuller in spirit, really, and sometimes extremely heavy grief can hold a spirit back from going on with what it has to do on the other side.

Ariel then informed me, "Your healing process is not yet over. You are to go on for further healing."

We alighted onto a sandy beach, and as we walked along the shore, Ariel told me to envision my inner child. Now, over the past few years, many of you have heard about getting in touch with your inner child. I, like many of you, didn't put much stock into the idea when I first heard about it. I thought it was just another new age fad. However, when I tried to reach her, she appeared, crouched in a corner of my mind, head hung down, and incredibly sad.

I looked out onto the vastness of the tumbling ocean as dolphins romped and played, making high arcing dives in and through the waves. Laughing, they called out to me to come romp with them. The child in me wanted desperately to run into the surf and play with the friendly creatures, but I held back, reminding myself that I was on this level to learn, not to play.

Ariel corrected my thinking immediately. "You are here to heal a part of yourself that you shut off and pushed aside all of your life. Why not release her now and let her come out into the light of love and acceptance?"

Happily, I ran into the crashing waves and felt the warmth of this magical sea upon my translucent skin. It felt lovely to kick my legs out from under me while being carried away from the shore on the top of a huge wave. I had a wonderful time with the dolphins and all sorts of other sea creatures who took me into the depths of their world. I found to my delight that I could breath under water as easily as above it.

The wonderment and joyfulness of this realm was breathtaking. Every creature upon this level was made beautiful by their pure joy of just being. They had no cares and no concerns. They were created to be playful and to bring the playfulness out in others.

When I was thoroughly played out, I sat upon the sun-warmed sand and made a sand castle that actually stayed together as I made it. Ariel sat with me, not saying anything.

In my mind's eye, I once again saw the little girl within. A young Diana stood in front of me. Looking directly into my eyes, she asked, "Why did you shut me away and discount my every need?"

Memories of growing up flashed through my mind. I had found, as a little girl, that it would simply never do to give in to my feelings of despair over situations within my life, especially those over which I had no control. No matter how much I cried, pleaded or begged, the adults in my world made decisions without my input. Wanting to be free of the despair that plagued me, I turned away from the weepy, sad part of myself, pretending to be settled with the changes adults were imposing upon me. I made a conscious decision as a child to pretend to be strong and brave, hoping that I would become so.

Picking up on this, the young Diana nodded her head in understanding as to why I had to leave her behind and grow up and away from her. However, sadness was still very much a part of the younger me.

Ariel stood up, taking hold of the young Diana's hand and my own. Walking along, Ariel told me, "Whenever you shun a part of yourself, you think you are freeing yourself from your hurt and pain. In reality, though, all you are doing is putting off the inevitable. Sooner or later, you will be confronted with your past pain and have to deal with it."

After letting that sink in, she continued, "Your inner child needs to be healed and loved by you. Accept the small, weak part of yourself that has been hidden from view for so long. It may be painful to explore that part of your personality because it will bring up past hurts. It was not the younger you that created the hurtful situations, however. That part of you needs to be rescued from her lonely prison and integrated into all areas of your life."

After another pause, she added, "The small child within you is waiting patiently for your open-armed welcome. Once the child within integrates with the adult you, she will emerge only in the areas that she feels comfortable in, such as when you create, play, dance and sing. She will bring a depth of fun and freedom to these activities as yet unknown to you."

Ariel then joined my inner child's hand with mine. I looked down at the small child gazing up at me, her eyes shining brightly with happiness and hope. How could I have turned away this small, beautiful, loving child during my lifetime?

I stopped walking, knelt down upon the sand and opened my arms wide to the child. She came to me, kissed my cheek and returned my hug. In the blink of an eye, she walked into my heart and soul.

Ariel put her arm upon my shoulder and said, "Humans do many things unintentionally. It is only through learning and guidance that we can correct our past errors and move onward."

I wish I had known that a hidden part of me was in such desperate straits while I was alive. Being a whole, integrated, healed person would have made living my life so much easier and much more fulfilling.

I urge you to take this information to heart and really think about your own inner child. If you need to incorporate your inner child into your life, do so now. By doing so, you will receive enormous benefits.

When you get to know your inner child, you get to know your self at your purest. I have always thought the love of very young children is the purest form of love. Very young children love their parents and friends unconditionally and without reservation. Adults teach children as they grow, however, to give or to withhold love on a reward–punishment basis. If a child is pleasing, it gets a portion of love but if, on the other hand, the child is displeasing, the parent's love is withheld. When we teach our children to love in that manner, we teach them to be critical of themselves also. This is how a child is imbued with low self-esteem and a poor self-image. For if a child measures love by the impossible yardstick of perfection, who is really worthy of love? Certainly not the imperfect child himself. The child then internalizes the knowledge that only the prettiest, most charming and most popular people are to be loved or admired, which to a child equates to being found unworthy.

We need to find a better way of teaching the concept of love to our children and to ourselves. Love cannot be meted out to only a few; it must be overflowing to all.

Have you ever noticed how contagious the laughter of a loved child is? You are in the presence of angels when a child is giggling and fully in love with life. Do not belittle him or make him feel foolish for his happiness. Let children be children. They have to be silly and goofy sometimes. Yes, they need to know self-control, and they will learn as they grow. But while children are small, let them express their playfulness fully and without limitation. Love your children for who they are. Do not disdain them if they do not look or act as you had envisioned that they would before they were even born. Do not set them or yourself up for failure in that way. The ache of not measuring up will last for his or her entire lifetime. Listen to your child play without him or her being aware that you are doing so. You will learn much about how the child has internalized his lifetime thus far. Children tend to act out what they live.

When I visited sick children in hospital, I found that those who recovered the quickest were the ones who had the best support systems. Their parents visited often and their nurses were loving and kind towards them. They seemed to like themselves very much and had very good attitudes towards their eventual healing and recovery. I would say that they felt deserving of good things for themselves.

Your inner child can take you on a tour of your own childhood and reveal to you what you need to do to improve your adult life. The input is valuable and very much worth taking the time to do.

I asked Ariel, "It was easy for me just now, but how can a living person get in touch with their inner child?"

"You should sit quietly and imagine yourself as the child that you used to be. Once the child is in view, invite it to speak to your heart and soul. The inner child within you may be hesitant to speak at first, depending upon how long you have hushed and ignored the child. Patience will be needed here just as it is in the healing of a living abused child. Your inner child needs to know that it can trust you before it will start speaking to you. Once it does, it may be afraid that you will shut it out once again because you will not like what you are hearing.

"If you find that you really are not ready to hear the child completely, tell it that you have to ask that it stops speaking for now but that you will welcome it later when you are more ready to hear its truth. Thank your inner child for trusting you enough to come out. This is very important, for if you do not, your next attempt may not be very successful."

The most important thing in the world is the emotional health of our children. We cannot move forward as a people until our children are loved and cared for. As our future leaders, policy-makers, and even prison inmates, our children are being prepared for their place within society right now. We can turn around many lives by touching them with love. How great it would be for the entire world to let all children know, regardless of social standing, that they are loved, needed and are worthy of everyone's respect and support so that they can grow up without harm, and in loving and nurturing environments. Every child deserves quality health care and a good, sound education. It is my hope that parents and policy-makers wake up soon to these facts.

Ariel and I stood looking out at the ocean of healing. The dolphins continued to flip and jump within their joyful paradise and I knew that I would be back here again to frolic with them. As they grinned their good-byes, I turned to Ariel and said, "I want to be able to come back here again."

She replied, "Soon, you will be able to come and go wherever you choose without a guide beside you."

I didn't want Ariel to ever leave my side. The desire to have her beside me did not come from fear of being alone but rather because I truly liked her and enjoyed learning from her immensely.

"Thank you for your affection towards me," she said. "All you ever have to do is think of me and I will come to you. I have been with you when you have been in spirit before, as well as when you have been alive."

Then, she added, "It's time to move on, Diana. Are you ready?"

---

[1]   Diana became involved with the AIDS cause when her close, long-time friend, Adrian Ward-Jackson, a governor of the Royal Ballet of which she was Patron, contracted the condition. He died on August

23, 1991. A frequent visitor to his bedside, Diana even took her two sons along so that they could experience the human side of the epidemic. Diana was criticized in certain circles for her compassion for AIDS victims. She countered with accusations that AIDS victims had been abandoned by society. Adrian's death clarified Diana's priorities and gave her a new, positive balance and inner calm. Caring for him against the wishes of the Court helped her throw off the shackles of the "men in gray."

Chapter 4

Onwards and Upwards

I FOUND MYSELF IN WHAT LOOKED LIKE AN ACCOUNTING DEPARTMENT. People with lengthy scrolls of dangling paper scurried to and fro, looking rather serious as they went about their duties. None looked younger than about 30 years of age. They all seemed to be quite educated and very intent on their missions.

The female spirits were shorter and rounder in shape than the males. Their faces were like those of the angels, very soft and full of love and light. They had hair of various colors, as do humans, that flowed below their shoulders. Since being in spirit, I have noticed that all females have long, flowing hair, not short, cropped, pulled up or back. The hair seems to be layered and cascades in gentle waves down the back.

I put my hand to my own hair to feel its length and found that I, too, had longer hair laid upon my shoulders in perfectly formed layers. Oh dear, I always wanted long hair, but thought that I must have looked frightful. There are no mirrors in heaven, thank God.

The men were taller and thinner than the women, yet had strong masculine facial features like that of Michelangelo's statue of David.

They were quite beautiful to gaze upon. However, unlike on the earth plane, one another's beauty was not celebrated here but it did stun me for a moment or two when I first gazed upon all these beautiful beings.

Ariel knew what I was thinking and said, "Diana, although appearances are not what matters in heaven, being here automatically brings out the beauty of each and every soul in every way."

Their gowns were plain white, unlike those of Ariel and the angels, which were of different colors. Curious, I asked, "Everyone here wears flowing gowns, but why are theirs white yet yours and the angels are of different colors?"

"Color speaks to newly-arrived souls, Diana. For that reason, guides and angels are colorfully presented so as to calm the soul when it first looks upon us. Scribes, however, have very little interaction with souls, other than when the soul is getting ready to reincarnate. By that time, the soul has been here for a while and no longer needs to be reassured of any spiritual presence it looks upon."

"Well, I certainly would not be apprehensive upon seeing a scribe as I was passing from life, I can tell you that!"

"Oh, Diana, you are too much!"

Ariel and I laughed together at my reference to an earthly point of view. Ariel pointed to a group of souls seated together in a circle. Smiling, she indicated for me to follow her.

Let me take a moment and describe for you what souls look like. Souls do not see one another physically as people with clothes, jewelry and makeup. We see the inner being. The form of the body is vaguely there, but the full attention is upon the facial features. The face becomes the image of the soul. Beauty of this sort you will never find upon the earth. Every soul looks different from all the others. It's a rather hard concept to picture in your minds, I'm sure. Trust me when I say that heaven is a place of total beauty, meaning that every single thing upon it is lovelier than anything you have ever seen before.

This level brought me together with others who had gone through the very same levels of learning as I had. Some had been in spirit for quite some time and were only just now being reunited with other souls.

The soul of a little girl called my name and I turned away from the circle of souls to see who it was. She came to me bearing a lovely bouquet of flowers, and said, "I have been waiting for you to join me on this level because I want you to give my family a message. I know how much I am loved and missed and I want my family to know that I will be reincarnating back to them."

I mentally asked her about her background.

"My name was Malissa and, ten years ago, I gave you a similar bouquet in London. A few weeks after giving you the flowers, my father, Daniel, and I were out driving and we had an automobile accident. I passed away but my father survived. When I arrived here, I gave myself the spiritual name Daisy after my favorite flower. I'm really happy about going back to my family again, and I will be called Daisy."

Ariel who had been sitting next to me in the group of souls explained, "Often, you choose to come back to the same groups of people you knew while you were alive. You do this for a number of reasons; sometimes the bond of love is so strong that you are eternally linked to an individual or group of souls and will relive many lifetimes with them, or, you have to keep experiencing conflicts with an individual or group until you resolve your conflicts peacefully so that your souls can progress spiritually."

"It would be preferable to your spirit guides," Nathan, the leader of the soul circle, interjected, "if your soul conflicts were resolved with both people being in agreement to the resolution. However, your guides know that not everyone is aware enough spiritually at this point in time and so, sometimes you must make your peace within yourself towards those who feel negative towards you so that you can release them and carry on without bitterness or anger. If you do not do this, you will spend more lifetimes with the very people you don't want to be around. Souls cannot progress when they are weighted down with resentment and hatred."

I joined the circle and would like to share with you what learned there. To release those you are in habitual conflict with or those who hurt you, imagine them within your mind looking back at you. Say to them that you do not want to carry the weight of your negativity towards them anymore. Tell them that they are no longer permitted to hurt you in any way. Put a white light around them and whisper out loud that you release them out into the universe with peace and forgiveness.

It's as easy as that. The next time you encounter them, you will see a big difference. The difference may not be in them, however, but you will see the change in yourself by how you react and respond to them.

The level of onwards and upwards gives souls a chance to meet with spirit guides other than their own, to discuss what they have absorbed thus far from the other levels of learning.

Communicating through thought, Nathan asked me, "Have you learned what your past fears and self-limiting beliefs are?"

I answered, "I have understood and conquered my fear of being alone and I now see that I have limited myself by forgetting previous soul lessons received when I had been in spirit before."

I added, "I had forgotten how beloved I was within the spiritual realm, and like many others, I had given in to mundane earthly thinking while alive."

The others within my group all agreed that they, too, had fallen short of the mark regarding the subject of fears and self-limiting beliefs. We all made a resolve to remember all of the spiritual teachings we had received over our many lifetimes and to put them into practice once we incarnated again.

Nathan went on to ask me, "Have you reconnected with your spiritual source?"

I answered, "Since entering heaven, I have not seen God, Jesus or any highly revered spiritual presence. However, I have felt the spirit of Christ next to me on every level I have been on. Feeling his tremendous power and love so near to me is reassurance enough of my eternal connection with him."

All in our group consented to full knowledge of our connection to the spiritual source that created us. Satisfied, Nathan disbanded the group. He told us to meet with our own spirit guide once again and continue on.

At this point, my soul revealed more about its goals for my most recent lifetime as Diana. I had spent much time in heaven between my last two lives. In the lifetime before the one as Diana, I had been a man and quite robust, even plump, if you prefer. That is why I chose to be on the thin side for this past lifetime, and why I was so concerned about my weight. Of course, I went to excess with the thinness, but realize now that I needed to do that in order to experience both excesses of body weight.

The time period for the previous life was during the colonization of America. My name had been Harry Hamilton and I had taken my family from England across the ocean. The only reason I bring this up is to say yes, I have been a man before, and yes, I have been rather large of frame, as well.

The reason for my not incarnating too soon after that lifetime was because I wanted to take my time and look about to evaluate all of my choices and to make sure that, at the soul level, I had what it would really take to speed me along in my growth. My desire then, as now, was to finish up with the business of living on earth so that I could retire into heaven and stay here once and for all. However, I have not yet reached that goal and will probably have to live several more lifetimes. That being the case, I set my mind to what it was that my soul needed to experience in future lifetimes.

After reflecting on that life as a man in the 18th century, I had found that being a man had given me certain privileges and rights that women and children did not have. So, after that lifetime, I had told Ariel, my spirit guide even then, that I wanted to come back as a woman of means who could and would help the less fortunate. I had reasoned that being a woman living in the 20th century would boost my growth and also that I would bring into this lifetime a wealth of experience and information that would help not only myself but others as well, especially women and children.

Ariel advised me that I would need to encounter misfortune myself, thereby igniting my soul's memory of past life hardships. In this way, I would not stray from my soul's chosen course. Ariel presented me with the opportunity to live a materially comfortable, albeit, emotionally disrupted life as a woman in England in the 20th century. I was also introduced at that time to Charles' soul. He and I exchanged ideas of how we could go about fulfilling my soul's desires as well as those of his soul. You see, he also has soul lessons that he needs to fulfill, as do we all.

Before we all incarnated, Charles and I decided together how, where and when we would meet and marry. We also met the two souls who would incarnate to be our children. The four of us all agreed as to what our purpose would be in the sharing of our earthly lives. Charles and I together agreed that we would explore what a loveless marriage was like and what loneliness was about. And, of course, Camilla's soul was in on our planning, since she was to play such a large part in our earthly lives.

In truth, Charles was as lonely as I was before, during and after our marriage. Of course, he and I expressed it quite differently to the outside world but, nonetheless, we were experiencing the same spiritual difficulties at the same time. The soul lesson we were to learn—but didn't—was to open our hearts and minds towards each other and to get past the hurts that we were inflicting on each other and on ourselves.

At this time, I can only speak for myself when I say that, while alive, I had turned away from that small voice inside me that was my soul gently reminding me that I had chosen this path and that I had all the qualities needed to successfully reach through Charles' coldness and aloofness. If I chose to, it used to whisper, I could resolve my doubts and confusions concerning our marriage without having to resort to embarrassing displays of childishness and public posturing. Instead of listening to that still small voice, I gave in to my ego and decided to hurt him back. Of course, I now see that I needed very much to get in touch with my soul but that I had shut down all lines of communication within myself and instead had looked outside to others for my own answers. On reflection, I now see that it was not a very good thing to have done.

When I had first arrived here, I asked myself if my most recent lifetime had been worthwhile or if it had been a complete mess-up. While I can say now that it certainly had its victories and successes, on the whole, it had not been lived quite as my soul had desired. Oh well, there is always next time.

As I joined Ariel, I asked her, "Why are all these scribes scurrying about with long lists of paper fluttering behind them?"

"Why don't you follow a scribe and see what they do?" she suggested.

Ariel knows that I learn best by observing. That's one of the reasons why I cherish her so, she knows me so very well.

Just then, a very short scribe with curly blonde hair came up to me, "Hello, I'm Patsy."

I looked at Ariel in surprise, wondering how Patsy knew I was looking for a scribe to follow. Patsy tilted her head back, looked up at me, put her hands on her hips and responded indignantly, "Even the littlest among the souls can communicate by thought."

Standing like that, she reminded me of a munchkin from the movie, *The Wizard of Oz*. I almost burst into laughter but controlled myself mightily and smiled instead. Teasingly, I asked her, "Were you eavesdropping on my thought conversation with Ariel?"

Her mouth turned into an "O" and her eyes flew open wide as she looked first at me and then at Ariel. For a moment I thought that I'd breached a rule of etiquette. Perhaps joking was not permitted with the scribes.

"The joke is on you, Diana!" Patsy said, giggling. "You should see your expression!"

Patsy and Ariel both enjoyed a laugh on me. I've always thought that turn about is fair play and, after my moment of shock, I giggled right along with both of them.

Patsy told me, "While you were talking with Ariel, Ariel had sent out a message amongst the scribes asking for one of us to come over to show you around."

The whole philosophy of mind communications was rather confusing to me at that moment. I asked Ariel how she could have been sending thoughts to me and to others at the same time without my awareness of it.

She told me, "Right now, you are concentrating on being able to communicate, as if you were learning a new language. It will just be a matter of time before you will get the hang of it all."

Ariel added, "Also, there are no secrets in heaven, therefore, there is no need for private conversations."

With that, she instructed me to go with Patsy to learn and observe. Patsy carried a scroll as did the other scribes. We sat down right where we had stood and she showed me her list.

"This is a list of all the souls on this level of heaven," she explained. "Everyone here will meet with a scribe and go through an intense step-by-step process of evaluation. I, like the other scribes, meet individually with everyone on my list to review in detail everything they have learned thus far."

"Why don't the soul's spirit guides meet with them? Why are scribes needed for this evaluation step?" I asked.

"We scribes are souls who wish to reincarnate but have to go through a bit more learning before we do. We saturate ourselves with all the details of reincarnation and the responsibilities that go along with it. Our mission is to get together with souls who had been prepared in all areas for reincarnation. We go over all the information the soul has been given since entering heaven. We ask the soul questions to gauge its absorption of the spiritual truths it has learned. Then we assess the soul's readiness on a checkpoint system from which it is deemed either ready or not ready for reincarnation at that time."

She added, "God's hand is in all of this from the very beginning. He and he alone knows the plan that he has for each soul. After God gives his permission for that particular soul to reincarnate, the soul's spirit guide goes over all of the details of the up and coming new life with the soul."

"Patsy, why is it up to God? Why doesn't the soul decide whether it is ready to reincarnate or not?"

"The decision is always left to the one in authority. God, the creator of your soul, would be the authority in this case." Patsy explained.

Then she asked me, "Can you remember all of the levels you have been to thus far? Now, imagine yourself reincarnating right now. Do you think you could do so and live more successfully then the last time, using the knowledge you've recently acquired?"

Knowing my propensity towards forgetfulness, I answered, "Probably not."

She stood up, nodding her head in agreement, and said, "We give the soul a chance to see for itself just how ready it is to reincarnate before passing it along to its own guide. Everyone here makes sure the souls are really ready to reincarnate."

At this point, I had quite a few questions for Patsy. "Why it is that so many of us are totally clueless as to how to live successfully if we have all been checked and rechecked before reincarnating?"

She explained, "When a baby is born, it has full spiritual retention. At about the toddler stage, children can sometimes be heard talking to what appears to be no one. In reality, they are communicating with their spirit guide and/or guardian angel. When the child is about five or six years of age, the spirit guide recedes into the child's subconscious mind in order to allow the child to focus on his or her earthly learning and experiences. Spirit guides know that it would be far too stressful for children to try and convince adults that they really are talking to a spirit and not an imaginary friend, so they quietly slip outside of the child's conscious awareness.

"When people get to their early teenage years and beyond, they start to become overwhelmed by all of life's struggles and concerns. Their spiritual knowledge is still there, of course, but they have forgotten to reconnect with God and their inner guide. Instead, they search in vain for answers and direction outside of themselves. Meanwhile, God and their inner guide wait patiently for them to look within for direction, comfort and support.

"Buried somewhere in the human mind is the knowledge of everything taught in spirit. Humans need to be reminded of this concept and that's why more and more spirits are reincarnating as higher level souls. The training and teaching that these souls have gone through while they are here is very intense."

Patsy finished by telling me, "You, too, will experience all of the highest levels of learning before you incarnate again."

"Were my previous lessons perhaps not as intense as this time or did I just not learn them satisfactorily enough? How many lifetimes have I lived, and did I keep repeating the same mistakes and negative patterns of behavior throughout each and every lifetime?"

Patsy's answer was not altogether strange or shocking, however I was a bit mystified by it.

"You have lived a total of fifty lifetimes. Everyone you knew well during your past lifetime has been with you in most of your other lifetimes. There have been lifetimes you have lived minus a few previously known souls, but those lifetimes were rather like a breather or a short break in order to obtain more experience and fortitude before you incarnated again with those with whom you continually have the most conflict."

I found Patsy to be a well-informed scribe. I was eager to absorb and learn what I could from her before going on with Ariel. I told myself to pay close attention to what Patsy was revealing to me. I know I am going to learn all of this as if my next life depends upon it, which in a manner of speaking, it does.

The roles in which souls interact with you change from lifetime to lifetime. Your mother during this lifetime may very well have been your brother during a past life. The point is that no matter how the souls are related or known to you, the difficulties you have with them must be worked out, or you will continue to relive painful lifetimes together again and again.

I was somewhat perplexed up to this point so I asked Patsy, "How can it possibly be fair for an individual to have to come back over and over again with a resistant soul who does not want to change or improve. Why should anyone have to suffer through many lifetimes trying to resolve difficulties with another who is determined to remain in conflict?"

Summing up what Ariel had told me before, Patsy made sense of the whole thing. "We are all on a spiritual journey. If another soul does not choose to go onward with us, we must be prepared to release them in order to allow both of us to progress upon our respective spiritual paths. Eventually, they will learn what they need to learn and perhaps reenter our lives once again. However, when they enter our lives again, they will have a greater understanding and love for us.

"The responsibility we have to ourselves is to allow only those who are true and loving towards us to remain within our lives. There is nothing wrong with trying to work things out with another. It is something altogether different, however, to allow anyone to hurt and belittle you, to make you feel less than what you are. Only by mentally, and sometimes physically, releasing those who are not soulfully good for you can you continue to grow in light and love."

Ariel had told me that to release a negative person or situation, one needs only to whisper away the negative influence coming from the people or circumstances involved. This is by no means a magic formula. It is, however, a direct communication from you to God. In essence, you are sending a message of what you will no longer accept or permit within your life.

The reverse is also true: whisper out into the universe and to God's ear what you *do* want to flow into your life. Let the universe and God know what you *will* permit.

It is important to remember that when you send messages out into the universe, the same things you are sending out will be reflected back at you. When you send a message from the heart to free yourself from anything restraining you or in any way hindering to you, you release from the bonds of restraint not only yourself but the other soul, as well. If, on the other hand, you send out negative, hurtful thoughts towards another, you will receive more negativity and hurt into your own life, as well.

Negativity is a roadblock. It is there to test and try your resolve. Don't forget that everyone, while they are on the spiritual plane, decides what negativity they will encounter while alive and sets up the necessary circumstances in great detail. All this is done for our successful ascent upon the spiritual ladder.

I told Patsy, "I would be happy to just be in heaven. I prefer not to be a spiritual climber. I did all the climbing I ever cared to do while alive."

She contradicted me immediately. "Remember when you were with the healing angels?"

I remembered the loving, sweet angels on that level. Thinking about them again filled me with gratitude for the healing kindness they had shown me.

Patsy then asked, "What did you choose at that time?"

I instantly got a mental picture of an angel inviting me to stay forever with her and the rest of the healing angels as a guide. Patsy didn't need to illustrate her point any further. When I was given the chance to just be in heaven, I turned it down in order to be free to go further along in my spiritual quest for more knowledge. My desire was, and always will be, to help as many people along the way as I can in their search for spiritual direction, truth and under-standing.

Suddenly, Ariel appeared next to me. "It is time to go on."

I hugged Patsy good-bye and told her, "Hurry up and reincar-nate because the world desperately needs your knowledge and in-sight."

She winked and said, "I'll do my best."

Ariel next took me to what she called "the level of mirrors"— what would prove to be a unique and mysterious place. When we alighted, I saw a cluster of souls looking intently into a mirrored lake. The moist, sweet air felt like silk. Trees and lush tropical flow-ers and plants teemed along the banks. Beautiful swan-like birds swam peacefully in the middle of the mirrored lake.

As Ariel and I took in the scene before us, I wondered what everyone was looking down at as they kneeled along the edge of the lake. Ariel told me to walk over to the edge, kneel down and peer into it. I soon found out!

Chapter 5

The Level of Mirrors

THE IMAGE OF THE BEING THAT WAS REFLECTED BACK TO ME WAS beautiful beyond description. No matter how hard I try to describe her to you, I will not do justice to the beautiful spirit. However, I *will* try because I believe that it is important for you to know what you may experience in your own afterlife.

The face looking back at me was human in that she had two eyes, a nose and a mouth, but that is where the similarities to a human face end. She had a breath-taking, unearthly beauty about her. Every single feature was perfectly balanced and aligned. There were no flaws about her skin, no freckles or any other kind of mark upon her face. As they gazed back at mine, her eyes expressed the most profound love and understanding imaginable—someone who knew me to my core and loved me beyond measure. I felt as if I could stare at her forever and be held captive by her enchanting look. She was peace and calmness personified.

I thought that perhaps she was an angel of great magnitude and beauty. I assumed that the angel was standing behind me, over-shadowing my own reflection. Looking behind me, however, I saw no one so I asked Ariel, "What's this all about? Who is she?"

She laughed merrily and said, "That is none other than your own soul."

In disbelief, I looked again at the lake's glassy surface and stared at the image peering back at me. The face was totally different from what mine had been in life. The coloring was the same, but other than that, the face was too angelic, sweet and mystical to be human. Pointing to the image, I said to Ariel, "I know my own reflection and that is not it."

Ariel smiled and said, "What you are seeing is not your physical reflection, but rather your soul's reflection. Those who do not realize their inherent goodness are sent to the level of mirrors to look upon their soul and to communicate with it."

I looked down once again into the reflection and asked my soul to speak to me. The water began to agitate, swirl and churn. One by one, images of people and places from my past came to the surface in rapid succession, each one viewed only for a moment before being pulled under to be replaced by another. The pictures blended together forming a collage of my past lifetime. The pictures of all of my family members, both by blood and by marriage, captivated me. I was literally watching all of the important people of my life pass before my eyes.

It was utterly fascinating and engrossing. I lost total awareness of Ariel and the other souls nearby as I viewed with wonder the pictures of my life. The collage stopped at the face of my dear papa. His face and features were just as I remembered them to be, as was his voice. I knew that he was somewhere upon this heavenly plane and I looked forward to the time when we would be reunited in spirit. I felt my heart leap at the sight of him. To see him once again filled me with happiness. Suddenly, his image began to speak to me.

"I'm sorry I didn't tell you often enough how much I loved you while you were alive. I know how much good you accomplished within so short a time, and I should have praised you much more vocally than I did. I ache to think of how I could have helped you more to cope when you were struggling so with the dilemma of your marriage. Far too many opportunities slipped through my fingers to take a firm stand with the press on your account. And will you also forgive me for the way I handled your childhood?"

I was a bit confused by it all. He had told me on numerous occasions how much I meant to him and as far as marriage counseling goes, he was no expert, that's for sure. I know that papa spoke to the press in my defense on a few occasions when they had bombarded him with questions pertaining to the state of my marriage. He always tried to be diplomatic with them and avoid offending any of the royals by his remarks. Basically he told them that Charles and I would work out our differences on our own and to leave us in peace so that we could.

When I was a child, papa adored me, of that I have no doubt. He was not an overly affectionate father, but he let us know that we were loved in many ways. It's hard put into words just how he let us know; it was just one of those things that all of us children understood. We never doubted that either of our parents loved us, even after their divorce when I was six years old.

I said to him, "I genuinely do not understand why you feel you were errant with me in any regard."

He answered, "When, following my death, I gazed upon my soul on the level of mirrors as you are doing now, my soul spoke to me. The knowledge it imparted hit home with my logical and emotional selves. I then understood that I had missed many, many opportunities to hug you children and tell you how much I loved you. Although heaven is not known for sorrow and tears, I wept when my soul revealed to me all the opportunities I'd let slip by."

He knew how uncomfortable I felt hearing him apologize to me, but he said, "I must do this for two reasons. First, I have to admit my failings concerning you so that my soul can be free of the guilt it carries. Second, you, Diana, must be presented with the chance to forgive me so that we will not carry past hurt and anger with us into our future lives together."

At that moment, I knew that what my father had said to me was the truth. I had been holding on to more hurt and anger towards him than I had dared to admit to myself. If I were to ever have a truly successful relationship with him in a future life, I must be truthful now about my feelings, both good and bad. I wanted to lay the past to rest and start afresh with my papa.

I told him, "My dear papa, you are right. My childhood had been unhappy because of the bitter divorce between you and mother. Yes, it was a lonely and fragmented childhood. But you did the best you could under the circumstances. I must admit, though, as a little girl, I felt abandoned by the two people I had needed the most. You were so busy, coming and going, being the

Earl Spencer, and my mother was busy in London living a totally different life from my own. I always felt there was nowhere for me to go where I could feel wanted and secure."

My father listened without defending himself. When I was finished, he told me the reasons why he had done what he had during my growing up years.

"Diana, I had been searching my whole life for someone to love me unconditionally, to accept me and my actions without reservation."

As he told me this, I nodded my head in agreement and said, "As I got older and a bit more mature, I realized as much."

He continued, "When someone I cared about became hurt or angry by the things I did, I felt they were rejecting me as a person. I did not see that they simply wanted me to be considerate and respectful of their love for me."

Upon reflection, Papa's reasoning was understandable and forgivable. As is true with all of us, the way he was raised colored his adult personality. Growing up, he had never been shown, nor was it clear to him as an adult, that love must be respected first and foremost in order for it to stay.

As a child, I did not understand why my parents couldn't work out their difficulties. Now, after reviewing my own life, I can see why they couldn't. When two people pull in different directions, something has to give—almost always the marriage. It's unfortunate that once we incarnate, we tend to forget so much of what we had learned on the spiritual plane. If we could remember more, we would surely save ourselves and others so much needless pain.

From my new vantage point on the spiritual plane, it is clear to me that to know your spirit, you must not be afraid of the truth within. Every one of us has moments of startling clarity and honesty about ourselves. At those moments, plug into that. Listen with an open mind. Do not close down the communication out of fear and disdain for what you are hearing. It sometimes sounds as if your inner voice is chiding you. Perhaps it is. Perhaps it is trying to stop you from going down a path of more pain and remorse. Self-knowledge is power. Let the knowledge within your soul liberate you from your self-imposed prison. Life was not given to you to be lived as a drudgery. It was given to be lived happily and joyfully.

I'm glad I had the opportunity to work out my differences with my very dear papa here upon the level of mirrors. I looked forward, more now than ever, for the time that he and I would be reunited in spirit to hug one another once again. My dear, dear papa, how I've missed you so.

All of my family members and friends, alive and in spirit, were presented to me one by one. I listened and chatted with each of them as we shared the thoughts and feelings we had not revealed to one another before.

Sarah Ferguson appeared before me and asked that I chat with her about the mutual jealousies that had come between the two of us while I was alive. I want to mention that she and I also shared many good times. She was another person who, in the beginning of our friendship, helped to heal me. We leaned upon one another for support and guidance in the face of Royal Court criticism and censure. Looking back at the situation, I can see how we really were more comic relief for one another than anything else. Our only defense against the men in gray of the Royal Court was to laugh about them behind their backs, something we did endlessly.

She and I agreed within our souls to live another lifetime together in the future and to repeat the conflict again so that we might resolve it once and for all and come into unconditional love for each other. I am glad that she and I will have another chance at working out our difficulties together. I think that she and I could have a close friendship in the future.

Rosa Monckton, my dearest and best friend, smiled so sweetly when she saw me and told me that her concerns for her daughter were not as great as before since she is coming along quiet well now. I told Rosa that I would always keep her daughter near to my heart and watch over her vigilantly. It was good to see Rosa again. We had shared so much of our hearts with one another and I told Rosa that she was one of the few people who had never let me down. Rosa said that she never would. She made an oath to me that she would oversee the charity that bears my name and that it would always help the people.

Paul Burrell was next to appear and I was so very glad to see him again, and he was most beside himself to see me. Paul was my confidante as well as my butler, and a very good and faithful friend.

"Paul," I said, "thank you so much for honoring me both while I was alive and in death, as well. You know you were always 'my rock.' "

His spirit told me, "Diana, because I loved you so much while you were alive, I will continue to uphold your memory and be the honored keeper of your most treasured secrets."

"My dearest Paul, I will keep you near me forever. You will know it is my hand that helps guide your life by what will unfold for you."

Hansat Kahn floated up after Paul. I apologized to Hansat for any embarrassment I may have caused him and his family. I admitted to being a bit pushy with him but, I explained, it was only because I had been so in love with him. I had entertained the thought of being married to him so fiercely that it had gotten in the way of my good sense when I had made statements about the two of us without his consent or agreement. Hansat told me that he had indeed loved me as well, but was bound by his Muslim faith to marry a Muslim woman. Before I bid his image farewell, I blessed him and told him that we would meet again within another lifetime.

Dear James Hewitt came up just then and asked my forgiveness for his writing of that ghastly account of our affair together. I told James that he had saved my heart at a time when it was very much in need of saving, and for that I would always be grateful to him. I gave him my forgiveness regarding the book and told him that he and I also had another lifetime to encounter together again. We both agreed at the soul level to be cast into a similar situation in our next lifetime together. It seems that I have to go around again with many of the people who, while meaning so very much to me, hurt me deeply. I hope I can come back stronger and not as vulnerable so that the connection between myself and all of these people will be happier and more rewarding for all of us.

One after another, my childhood friends appeared and told me how they had all been fooled at first by my demure manner, but upon getting to know me, they had all been shocked at the pranks that I could successfully pull off. They had laughingly called me a wicked child. I was forever running into the house with all sorts of creatures that I had found and had wanted to give a home to. I had let my hamster out of its cage on many occasions to give it freedom, much to the household staff's chagrin. The staff were tremendously patient with me, however, and put up with me quite wonderfully, even when I constantly begged for sweets to feed my pals. I know that I doubled their duties many times.

I particularly remember my chat with Carolyn Bartholomew, one of my closest childhood friends and flat-mates. To my friends, I am sorry that there is not enough room here to name you individually, but be assured that I enjoyed our time together in the mirror.

The conversations with my family were quite a bit more intense, however, as well as terribly emotional. We talked about the jealousies, the hurts, and the blame that we all carried within our hearts towards one another. I had wanted my sisters, my brother and my parents to rescue me from my hideous marriage but they had all told me basically to put up and to shut up. True, my brother and one of my sisters were much more sympathetic to my plight, but still they insisted that I make my marriage work. As if I could have pried Charles and Camilla apart!

I joked with them that if I could have done so, I would have had Camilla thrown into the tower and banished forever. The nickname I had for Camilla—"the Rotweiller"—aptly described the woman, I thought. Rotts are famous for stalking their victims while the victim is unaware of being stalked. Then, with the element of surprise, the beast attacks suddenly and violently, rendering its poor victim defenseless. This is what had happened to me concerning Camilla. The only previous knowledge I had of her was that she was an old girl friend of Charles and, as far as I knew when I came on the scene, they were just good friends. What frustrated me so much was that I had unknowingly walked into a marriage that the men in gray knew was a sham from the start. They knew about Camilla and yet they kept it a secret from everyone, including me. I was scrutinized up and down because a marriage partner of suitable lineage and purity had to be found for Charles. I met all their criteria, and that's all that mattered to them. They didn't care a whit about what I was unknowingly walking into.

My family could not comprehend my anger at the irony of it all. I told them that for my marriage to be mended, Charles must give up Camilla and cooperate with me by going into marriage counseling. It wasn't up to me alone to fix our marriage. Although I felt very much alone while married to Charles, I was, in fact, his wife and mother to his children, and I felt that he and I should have worked out our difficulties together. Apparently I was alone in thinking this way. I felt as if I had lost my moorings to my family while

I was going through the farce of my marriage. I knew that I was in the ring without a coach or guide and that made me very angry and upset at all of them.

Sick and tired of hearing my rantings and ravings, my family had retreated from talking to me about the whole sordid mess. They told me that there was nothing any of them could do about it and that I had married not only Charles, whom at the time was thought of as the future king of England, but the royal family as well.

Getting out of the marriage would be costly and quite sticky, not to mention the fact that I would lose so much, perhaps even my precious boys. I felt that I had no real choice. I was in this mess alone and would have to think of a way on my own to liberate myself without losing my boys. I knew that to lose them would be to lose my life. I would have literally died a lot sooner if they had been taken from me

If asked, my family will answer honestly that they have had dreams in which I have talked to them many times over about what is mentioned here. How much of the dreams they will remember, I don't know. I do know that their subconscious minds will remember everything that was said and will store the information for future use.

When the time comes for us to live lifetimes at the same time, my part of the guilt, blame and hurt feelings will not be carried back with me into our future relationships. They must also wholeheartedly agree to let all of these hurts and misunderstandings go if they wish to be on firmer footing with me in any future lives that we have together.

I know that my spirit was healed tremendously from my chats with my family members, and I hope theirs were as well. I look forward with great excitement to living together with all of them in a future life. After clearing up the misunderstandings between us, we all saw that love remained. It had always been there and, for the most part, we knew that, but it had so much rubbish piled on top of it that it was nearly suffocated. Now that the refuse has been cleared away, I believe our paths will be much clearer and we will be able to go forward together as a healed unit.

I was surprised that I did not encounter my beloved grandmother, Countess Spencer, within the reflective pool. I do not know why that was, however, I was to reunite with her later and we had a wonderful time together.

The next to appear within the lake was my darling Dodi. He looked tired and as if he had been crying. This startled me to no end because, for me, heaven was a paradise on every level, except for Pebble Island, of course.

"Darling, what's going on with you? Where are you at this moment?"

I had to know. He looked as if he were still a living person, with no angelic soul glow to his image. My mind could not conceive of what he must be going through. He said nothing at first. We just looked at one another. The sadness in his eyes was unspeakable and heart-rending. He was wracked with sobs but finally began to speak. He spoke through thought as did every one else, so I could no longer hear his accent. I suppose he couldn't hear mine, either.

"Let us go back and redo our last night together. Perhaps take a different route. Or not even go out at all."

Tears filled his eyes and spilled down his cheeks. It alarmed me greatly that he was still in so much pain. I asked him again, "Where exactly are you?"

"I am on a level that is trying to teach me of forgiveness."

"Trying? I don't understand, darling, what do you mean by *trying* to teach you? There are excellent teachers up here, I simply don't understand."

"Yes, trying," he replied softly. "I just can't get past it all, Diana."

His spirit cried out for me to help him through this. I desperately wanted Ariel to help him and turned to her to ask for her guidance. She replied, "Dodi has been put on a level where he has to talk with souls who have been victimized in all sorts of ways while alive. All of this is to help him to see that a soul sometimes gets hurt and perhaps loses its earthly life due to the cruelty of others. But very importantly, these souls have chosen to forgive whatever the circumstances of their death so that they can move on and progress within the spiritual realms. However, he cannot see why he should forgive anyone."

Turning back to Dodi's reflection, I asked him, "Why can you not forgive?"

"How can you ask me why, Diana? You and I were to have had a life together. Don't you remember anymore?"

"Of course I remember but we can also be with one another up here as well. Perhaps it would be better up here for us, darling. You see, in spirit, we are far more protected than we ever were in life. There will be no interference, no cameras, no gossip. Here we can fly side-by-side and experience this beautiful place together."

"Oh, Diana, I so want to be with you again."

Dodi looked directly into my eyes and smiled for the first time since I had seen his reflection upon the lake.

"Diana, to be with you is worth all of my efforts to forgive. I will try. I want you to fly to the level of forgiveness and swoop me up."

Knowing the level of Dodi's determination, I know that we'll be together again shortly. This time, however, no one or anything will separate us. As his image dissolved back into the lake, I wished him, "Godspeed, my darling."

You may be wondering why our souls would take us from the earth plane just six weeks after we realized our love for each other. I had known that he was going to ask me to marry him. However, I also knew that Dodi was a playboy and I did not want another disastrous marriage. I was frantic not to hurt him and so I told him that I would consider a proposal of marriage if he asked me, yet I also knew that I could not have married him. I was quite stuck at that time as to how to get out of this situation without hurting him. It is quite clear to me now that our souls timed our deaths so as to avoid me hurting him.

When the faces stopped coming to the surface, I took a pause and wondered if I had been to this level following any of my previous lifetimes. If so, had I been open and honest with myself and with the others within our shared lifetime when I had gazed into this lake? I once again looked upon the lake. The angelic face of my own soul reappeared asking, "Look directly into my eyes."

I did so and knowledge of myself being upon this spiritual level many times before flooded my mind. I knew then that I had resisted this most important level of learning every time it had been presented to me. I had never completely opened up to it as I was doing now. In the past, it had been too painful for me to explore and then admit to the negative feelings that I had harbored towards those of my family and friends. Admitting to unpleasant feelings towards family members had always seemed like betrayal to me. Through soul-searching, I discovered just how fervently I had embraced the idea of loyalty in regards to my family members throughout each of my lifetimes.

My soul said to me, "As a spirit matures, it learns to become more honest with itself. Sometimes this can take many incarnations, as is the case with you."

My soul then showed me one of my earlier incarnations and in a way I cannot explain, I found myself *inside* the image. The view before me was dark, cold and forbidding. I was a young servant girl inside a bone-chilling castle. Animal skins hung upon the walls, roaring fires sputtered and spat inside huge fireplaces, and everywhere reeked of the nasty smells of rot and decay. My dress was no more than sackcloth, stitched and restitched. It was as filthy as the place I was in.

The Diana part of me no longer wanted to stay in this cold, frightening place of ongoing abject misery, so I asked the beautiful reflection to return and make this horrible picture go away.

To my relief, the angelic face appeared once again, reminding me, "This is not something from outside of you, but your own soul appearing, willing you to probe into my vast wealth of knowledge and guidance."

Before asking my soul any questions about the lifetime I had just viewed, I sat back to contemplate the enormity of the fact that my soul could and would communicate with me. To be able to tap into that inner resource was somehow still unbelievable to me. I had been told again and again that it was possible and that I had been here before to do just that. A part of me wanted to learn all about myself and all of my lives and yet a part of me wanted to stop right here and now. The unknown gives me a chill because I don't know if I really want to see what is hidden.

When I realized how I had been wrestling and arguing with myself, I realized that it was precisely at this moment every time before that I had backed down from listening to my soul speak. Out of fear, I had always fled this level. I decided to go forward this time. I felt a rush of anticipation for what was to be revealed, as well as more than a bit of fear.

My soul said, "You were a scullery maid in a castle for a war-loving, perverse English sovereign. It is the twelfth century. Your mother is also a servant within the castle. Your father is a stable hand. You sleep in a tiny room just off the dungeon-like kitchen. There is no home life for you since you are at the king's beck and call every single moment of the day and more often than not, into the night."

Suddenly I was back in the castle and could sense my terror of the king, and of everyone else, as well. I was permitted only within the kitchen and huge dining hall. My hands were chapped and raw. Looking at the face of my mother, I could see how ill and tired she was. She was probably only about 25 years old, but looked 90. Death seemed a welcome reprieve from the life that the servants lived within this castle.

I asked my soul, "What was the purpose of this life?"

"You wanted and requested a life of total servitude for all the days of that incarnation."

"Why on earth would I request a life like that? Who in their right mind would choose something that awful for themselves? Did I know before reincarnating what time period it would be?"

The hellish castle disappeared as my soul appeared in the lake's reflection to answer my questions. "You requested that life to experience the lowliest of positions before any social reform. You had no rights and there was no aid or programs for people who needed assistance. To be sure, there were earlier time periods in which you could have incarnated in order to experience a lowly position, but this one would speak to your soul the loudest."

My soul, as does yours, knows that it needs to live through many lifetimes in order to fulfill its destiny. Souls often choose earlier periods of world history to experience strife, political upheaval, famine and tribulation because in those earlier ages of human history, people were less soulfully aware of the atrocities of inhumanity towards the lower classes. Cruel servitude and even slavery were often the norm in many societies.

Those earlier cultures provided many opportunities to experience life in ways that make us stronger, more compassionate towards others and better equipped to handle adversity in our future lives when we would be given positions of power and authority. The soul is born into a time period where it will undergo much strife. This happens many times over before it is elevated to a higher position in a future life. It must learn its lessons well for, in later lives, it will have increasing levels of authority and must not misuse it.

An excellent example is Adolf Hitler. His soul had already suffered many lifetimes of imprisonment, starvation and painful death, and yet he chose to inflict the pain of his earlier lifetimes upon millions of people once he occupied a position of authority and power. Rest assured, he will have to repeat countless lifetimes of pain and suffering once again, and he may never again have another chance at leadership. However, it is not for his enemies to decide, but up to his God and his soul.

The painful life lessons my soul had set up were intended to teach me that everybody, regardless of their station in life, has feelings, hopes and fears. In that oppressed medieval lifetime, my soul and spirit guide were preparing my soul for the eventual position of power that I was to have. Apparently, it had been necessary for me to start at the bottom, so to speak. I learned my lesson of total and absolute servitude very well. I never again had to repeat a life lesson similar to that one, thank God.

Living the servant's life of extreme poverty, isolation and hopelessness was so devastating to my spirit that since that lifetime, my soul has taken on the task of becoming a nurturer, healer and advocate for the disadvantaged. The sadness and despair of that servant child is branded within my soul's memory forever.

Many times, people say they feel compelled or called to perform a certain task that may defy explanation. This is so because of their soul's memory of a particularly moving past life experience. Not all past life experiences are negative; some may have been quite joyful and fulfilling. Whatever the case, you will be motivated by your spirit to do what you were born to do.

A lot of people at this moment in time haven't a clue about what they are supposed to be doing. Your soul is much more prepared and knowledgeable than you may give it credit for. It waits until the right moment in time to nudge you towards your destiny. Of course, you could enter into meditation with your soul and ask it just exactly why you were sent here and what it is that are to do. However, be prepared. The answer you may receive may surprise you and cause you to totally reexamine your life up to that moment.

Whatever your mission, however, every one of you has the chance to make this lifetime more loving and healing than the last, both for yourself and those around you. Personally, I think that sums up reincarnation rather nicely. However, I urge you not to wait until after death. The real opportunity is while you are still alive.

As my soul took me through every incarnation I had ever lived, it became apparent to me that each lifetime leads up to the next one. I was surprised to find out that lives are not just randomly passed out to us. They are logically designed and carefully orchestrated. The obstacles encountered and overcome during a lifetime help to prepare us for the next set of challenges and hurdles that are sure to come within our next lifetime.

A few of my lives had not been lived successfully. During those lifetimes, I either had caused my own death or had lived a life of pain and regret because I had not yet realized that I needed to listen to my soul in order to nurture my spirit. I learned that I had chosen many lifetimes of unhappiness, want and misery, and regret to say that it took a few too many lifetimes before my actions successfully demonstrated the soul teachings I had received while on the spiritual plane.

Patsy had mentioned that I'd already had 50 lives, and of those, Ariel had told me that, in 25 of them, I was a member of a royal family, however distantly. My soul told me that many of those lifetimes had been ones in which, I'm sorry to say, I had been given privileges of wealth and had not shared well with the less fortunate.

In others, however, I had not been wealthy but had desired wealth alone, spending many precious lifetime hours wishing my wealthier counterparts ill will. In those lifetimes, I had been a servant or had been, in one capacity or another, beneath the social standing of the upper classes.

Living like that had been hard but I had chosen my thoughts. Instead of concentrating on how I could have improved myself in any little way, I had concentrated on how much I hated everyone above me. I am glad that today there is so much information available about the relationship of thoughts and manifestation. What we think, we bring to ourselves. It's simple, really. I could have turned around any lifetime of unhappiness if only I would have allowed my soul to remind me that I was only a victim within my own mind. It wasn't until this past lifetime that, just before I died, I finally allowed that soul-held knowledge to come to the surface. I would have to say, then, that the last three years of this most recent lifetime had been my most victorious time of living. Ever.

I had learned that in order for a person to live a life successfully, the spirit inside needs to be looked after, cared for and nourished. By listening to your soul, loving and honoring the spirit inside of you and learning all you can about your spirituality, the time you spend in the spiritual realm after you pass from the earth will be mostly enjoyable. It will be as if you are simply recharging your batteries and happily preparing to reincarnate once again.

I thought I could get by in my life by being a good person and doing what I thought was right. I found out, however, that no matter how hard I tried to please, there was always someone who was unhappy with me. During the last few years of my life, I realized that in order for me to be happy and at peace with my self and my decisions, I had to let go of my obsession with worrying that I was upsetting and letting down those I knew well. I took the gamble and began living my life without caring about what my detractors said about me. I lived as if I were in charge of my destiny. The way my life changed for the better amazed me. I still cared about and loved people, but the big difference was that I chose very carefully who to keep close to me and who to let go.

What helped me best and gave me the most knowledge about this was when I studied many different religions. For a time I consulted astrologers and psychics. While they helped somewhat, I never felt that I received all of the answers I needed. However, studying religions such as Islam opened my eyes to many universal truths. I found that no matter what the religion, the message is always the same—love yourself first and foremost and then you will be able to love others.

As I said earlier, I am not bitter or resentful that, after finding true happiness, I was taken from the earth. I am just glad that it happened while I was still on the earthly plane. After all, how many people can say they've had even one solid year of their life filled with almost total happiness and fulfillment?

I know that my future incarnations are going to be so much the better for all of the soul lessons I have been through. I had met my soul and found the true value of myself. I had not backed down but had embraced the truth of me for the first time since my creation. The liberation was immense. I was free.

Chapter 6

The Level of Tears

PEOPLE SEEK SUICIDE AS AN OPTION WHEN THEIR LIFE SEEMS TO press in on them and they can see no other way out. A few months after Charles and I were married, I was in exactly that situation. I had gone from a carefree, fun-loving young woman to the Princess of Wales, totally under the control of the Court. I had suddenly become a possession of the crown.

My life was in tatters. Camilla loomed everywhere I looked, and Charles simply would not or could not understand why that bothered me. I begged him to stop seeing her and to help me cope, but he steadfastly refused, telling me to pull myself together and to get on with it.

In a desperate attempt to win his attention, I told him that I would take my own life. His reply to me—that he was going riding—told me that he couldn't have cared less at that moment whether I lived or died. So I threw myself down the stairs at Sandringham. In other cries for help, I would cut myself and stab myself with sharp objects, but none of these antics helped my marriage and, to quite a large degree, made it considerably worse. Charles lost any semblance of patience and tolerance he had for me with each desperate and destructive act I committed against myself.

I have met many people on this side who successfully committed suicide, and the unanimous verdict amongst all of them is they regret it intensely. Their cry for help backfired horribly, and they actually died.

Here's what two of them had to say.

"My name is Monica. I am 13 years old. I lived with my parents, brother and sister in Salsbury, Michigan. I took my mom's anti-depressant pills, all 30 of them. I put handfuls in my mouth and kept gulping water until they were all gone. I was overweight, or at least thought I was, and lonely. I had some acne that I thought at the time was the only thing people saw when they looked at me. I had told my school counselor how unhappy I was but couldn't tell him why. I couldn't put it into words. I know now that I was suffering from severe depression.

"My mom and dad were not really into thinking that kids could be depressed. They had me when they were in their late thirties and I always felt that I was their "oops child." My brother and sister were smarter than me and not a pain like I was. I thought I would do everyone a favor by taking my life. When I think about it though, I didn't really know what I was doing. I mean, I didn't think of death as permanent. I don't know why, I guess I just wasn't thinking, as my mom would often say.

"I want to tell my parents and brother and sister that I'm sorry that I took my life. I'm also sorry that we couldn't talk to each other. I've learned a lot since I've been up here, but I have to tell you that I'm not totally at peace. I know the pain I caused but I also know that the pain I felt wouldn't have just gone away on its own. I needed help, mom and dad. Telling me to stop moping around and to snap out of it didn't make me any better.

"I know you miss me, and mom, I know that you're sorry that you weren't there for me more. What can I say? I don't have all the answers and I'm still not positive about what I could have done to help myself. I mean, I just didn't have anyone to turn to at all. My guide, Brighton, tells me that I did. He says I could have opened up more and been more honest and all. He says that I have to learn up here what I didn't down there. I have to learn how to rely on my own soul's knowledge, and I have to remember what the angels and Brighton are teaching me. The angels are so nice to me and they're very pretty, too.

"I have to accept the fact that my life and death were my responsibility. I still need to learn about forgiveness and things like that. I am trying to forgive you, mom and dad, but I still hurt inside. I didn't think anyone hurt inside in heaven, but I do. I'm not allowed to fly around like I thought I would up here. It's not a picnic, it's more like being in school all the time. I'm not tired or anything like that, I just want to have fun again. Brighton says that I have to come back and try a life again. He said that since I took my life, I don't get to stay up here too long, so there's no time for me to fly around and stuff like that. I just have to learn and learn and learn. Maybe being alive again wouldn't be too bad after all.

"Diana asked me to say something to all you down there who are hurting like I was. All I can say is talk to someone, anyone. Don't stop until you get help. I know that I didn't do that because how could I tell anyone what I was feeling? How could I say, "Hey, I hate being alive"? What would people have thought of me? That's why Brighton says I need to learn more—this is what he's talking about. I still have lots to learn and I'm trying to. But you who are still alive, hang in there. Heaven is okay, but not what you think it is. It's not a paradise if you kill yourself. But if you wait until God tells you to come up here, then it's a paradise. If you don't wait to be invited, you'll have to go back and try living again and you won't get to fly and have a blast up here. God loves you and all, but it's like you're forcing him to take you before he's ready to when you kill yourself. Brighton's calling me back, so I have to go. It was nice to be able to tell everyone how I was feeling. That helped me a lot. I hope what I said helps people, too."

"Hi. My name's Paul. I killed myself by driving while I was drunk. I wanted to die anyway and didn't care how. I meant to kill myself and not anyone else, but I did. When I left my house that night, I didn't know it would be for the last time. I was thinking of ways to die all of the time. It just worked out that I died the way I did. If the accident hadn't killed me, I would have tried taking my life by some means, anyway.

"I lived in Rock Hill, North Carolina with my mom and stepdad. One night I went out drinking with my friends. I was 18 and should have known better. My mom is a member of MADD now. My stepdad doesn't talk too much anymore. He used to be so funny, too. My real dad said that it's my mom's fault that I was drunk, 'cos he said she never gave me any rules to stick to. I wish he wouldn't say that to mom. She's so sad all the time and feeling guilty. Mom, it's not your fault.

"I'm sad for all of you. I'm sad for me. It's like Monica said, it's not fun and games up here and not only that, but you have to witness what your suicide did to your family and friends, too. Yeah, we watch you guys struggle everyday with your pain and guilt. I don't want my family to feel guilty. You told me every time I went out the door to be careful. I didn't know that, when someone dies while driving drunk, it's considered a suicide. Well, I mean in my case, it was like suicide because I'd wanted to die anyway and succeeded, but I killed the guy in the car that I crashed into, too. I didn't mean to take anyone else with me when I died. It was an accident. I can't say too much more, 'cos I get too emotional and then I can't concentrate on anything my guide tells me.

"My guide's name is Pete and he says that before I come back to earth, I'll have to go and meet with the guy I killed. I'm not looking forward to that 'cos I don't know what I'll say to him other than I'm sorry. Sounds pretty lame to me; imagine how it'll sound to him. Have to go and talk to my guide now. I'm sorry, really, really sorry, everyone. Please forgive me."

Paul and Monica were very brave to share their stories with all of you. They have not been up here long, but their guides felt that it would help both of them enormously to chat with all of you. It is Monica and Paul's intent to learn and grow in spiritual truths while they are here in heaven and I applaud their great effort. I was quite surprised myself to hear that they are not really resting in peace, however. They are certainly being loved and guided while here, but not coddled. They did not tell their stories to cause further pain, but to help other young people who may be considering taking their lives. It is quite a different level, this. It is pretty here but not as spectacular as some other levels of heaven have been. I wish they could swim with the dolphins and laugh and play as I do, but their guides tell me they are not to be rewarded. It's very sad really because I for one have always felt that fun is an important part of the learning process. However, I trust their guides explicitly and know that they have the soul's best interest in view at all times.

Anyone who commits suicide will be shown love and mercy, of course, but they will also be shown the effect their suicide had upon everyone they had known and loved.

This level of heaven is called the Level of Tears; not for the tears of the spirits but for the tears of those they left behind on earth.

I am finding that heaven is a place of contrasts just as earth is. Nothing is completely understood by a spirit until it has been put through a learning process, again, much like an earthly school system. The only difference here is that you do not get brow-beaten if you do not understand or pick up quickly. The angels and guides are loving and kind. They can be stern, but their sternness is not filled with contempt or anything derogatory or in any way insulting towards the spirit who is learning.

I have met and talked with many other spirits who also committed suicide but as adults. They are treated very similarly to the children. The difference, however, is that the adults must stay here longer with their guides as they have much more to unlearn.

I agreed to come to this level without Ariel to test my mettle, so to speak. I do not like it here because there is a total absence of laughter and fun. This is very solemn work for the souls and the guides, but it is best for the souls to get on with the learning and reincarnate. They don't seem to want to leave right away, however. They want to feel safe and protected for a bit before taking a deep breath and being sent back to earth as newborn babies. I can understand somewhat, but these are mostly children after all, and my mothering instinct is still intact. I want to hold them all within my arms and tell them that they are beautiful creations of God and that they can stay with me up here where no hurt will ever come to them ever again.

I can see that I am not strong enough yet for this type of work, so I will go now. Before I do, I will visit with each and every soul upon this Level of Tears and hold them close to me for a moment, then bid them a loving fare-thee-well. I will whisper to each one that no matter how long and hard the journey, they are to remember that they are loved and guided from above. I will tell each one of them that I want them to place this knowledge deep within their hearts and souls to carry them through the hard times that are sure to come when they live a life again.

Before I came to this level, Ariel told me that all suicides will have to come back to another lifetime of abuse or loneliness or whatever it was that they had sought to escape when they took their life. This sounded outrageously unfair to me until Ariel explained that we are all equipped to handle the various cruelties of life, but we must reach down deep for this knowledge and pull it out of ourselves in order to overcome. Oh, if we could only remember, how much pain and sadness we could spare ourselves and others.

In closing this chapter, I would like to give the following message to our leaders and policy-makers:

Please, please look at all the lives lost due to ignorance, homelessness, hunger and abuse. Money is available and at the ready to help every person who suffers from these ills. The world must sit up and take notice. We need to teach everyone that they have value and are worthwhile. Until we do that, you will keep losing your loved ones to suicide. People who think they have nowhere else to turn will turn to suicide. It's that simple. Teach our children while they are in school that they must support and comfort one another. That they must be kind and gentle also to those spirits who are not as strong as they are. That we all depend upon one another for our survival.

Finally, let me say to all the parents and teachers of today that you need to start listening more with your hearts and with your eyes. When your child or pupil is in a bad way, you can feel it and see it. It hangs all about the child. Do not be afraid of intervening or appearing nosy. By doing so, you will have saved a life and will also have spared yourselves and the child continuing grief. If you are an abusive parent, please get help immediately. The well-being of both you and your child hangs in the balance at this very moment.

For adults who are in bad straits, please talk to someone and let people know that you are hurting. It is when you reach out in hope and trust that someone will reach back. Do not give up. Suicide is not painless. What you hope to escape from you will encounter again. So, face whatever you must in this lifetime and grow stronger and more compassionate because of it. That's the whole point really.

Chapter 7

Death with Dignity

MANY OF THE AIDS PATIENTS I VISITED IN HOSPITAL PASSED away while I was still alive. I have been reunited with most of them up here on the level of healing. I was invited back to this level by the healing angels after I had completed my first round of learning on the other levels because they told me that I am now better equipped to engage in counseling the other souls here.

Archangel Raphael himself came to me as I was observing with Ariel how it is that little babies are welcomed into heaven, and invited me to go along with him to the healing level. Before I tell you about the healing level, I want to take this opportunity to talk to you about your departed precious babies.

I have learned something so very fascinating that if I had not been in heaven when I learned it, I might not have believed it myself. It is this: The souls of tiny babies who die while in the womb to within the first six months of life are swiftly carried back into heaven where they are refreshed and healed and then reincarnate again to experience this very same thing once more. It is all done very quickly. They have volunteered for this very hard experience for several reasons.

First and most importantly, when a baby dies, its short life teaches us that nothing, including life itself, is promised to anyone and that we must value life and celebrate it to its utmost. The death of a tiny baby will touch anyone even remotely connected to the mother and father. It will make people cherish the children they already have even more so.

Secondly, these wonderful souls do much to further research and study in the areas of medicine, grief and recovery. For this purpose, these souls incarnate as infants over and over again in order to partake in human life, no matter how briefly. I think of them as the most brave of all the souls because I know, from what I had read before coming here and from what Ariel has told me, that being born is painful. The powerful contractions hurt not only the mother but the baby, as well.

These souls are selfless in that they go through the pain of birth many times over in order to bring their teachings to human lives. Not only is birth painful, but then they may also have birth defects that are unpleasant for them to endure, such as heart conditions, lung failures and many other types of maladies. After a time, these souls sometimes do change their spiritual minds and decide to in-carnate so as to experience a full lifetime. These are the people who thoroughly enjoy life no matter what is thrown at them. I'm sure everyone has met at least one person who is perpetually cheer-ful. Well, it could be they've had a few go-arounds as infants with early deaths and have learned to value and cherish every bit of life.

It is with much fanfare that these tiny souls are welcomed back into heaven. The powerful archangels themselves come for the souls of these brave infants and fly with the babies held lovingly close to them up into heaven once more. They are then gently caressed, rocked and loved back to spiritual healing by a multitude of angels. I watch with much joy in my heart at how beautifully the angels care for their small charges. Nothing in heaven is valued more.

Raphael, the archangel of healing, wants me to talk about the aborted babies of the world. Once again, it is the will of the infant's soul to endure the experience of abortion. These tiny teachers allow this to happen to them because they want to raise human awareness to a greater level.

The mother of the aborted baby needs to learn not only about self-forgiveness, but about forgiveness of others as well. She may be angry at herself for getting pregnant and also at the man who impregnated her, and to compound matters, perhaps he has even deserted her in her time of great need. She then has to overcome strenuous objections regarding her choice from her family and from society, as well.

There is much we can learn from abortion. Most important is that when we are faced with an impossible situation, we should look to our guides, to God, and to our inner knowledge, and not believe that we are forced into making a decision that we know in our hearts we will regret. Far too many women have ended their babies' lives because they felt they had no other alternative. However, the guilt from the abortion will often be like a noose around the woman's heart for the rest of her lifetime. Forgive yourselves, dear ones—you are greatly loved and forgiven. You need only to connect to the tremendous love that encircles you daily to know this. Reach out for that love and guidance, ask for it to be made known to you, and your spirit will be healed as well as your heart.

Once humankind learns how to care for every individual and welcome every child into the world, no matter what its social class, no woman will ever again have to make the agonizing decision of whether she can afford to have her baby or not. However, there are some women who use abortion as if it were birth control. All I have to say regarding that is: Stop this instant! You are amassing a huge karmic debt against yourselves. When you have a large amount of karmic debt, you will have to live through countless lifetimes where you are constantly the victim in order to repay or balance out the debt you are building up. Do not be careless with life—yours or anyone else's.

I would also like to add that babies who live a few days to two years are not going to reenact this over and over again. These souls instead live a short life in order to make a profound impact upon at least one person's life. It may be on the mother or the father, or another family member or close friend.

Further, when a baby older than six months dies, the person who is most affected will have a life-changing experience due to the baby's life and death. Of course, everyone who knew the baby will be affected but it is usually only one who will dramatically have his or her life changed.

For example, that person may suddenly decide to become a pediatrician or a nurse, or want to start a foundation in order to care for many children who have whatever disease it was that claimed the baby's life.

In cases where the baby had been abused or dumped off somewhere, an awakening will occur within the community, be it city, state or country. After a story comes out about a baby's tragic death due to abuse and neglect, people become more aware and much more caring of children. Do you see what is happening here?

A soul decides before incarnating what its purpose or mission will be. In the case of baby abuse or cruelty, the soul's mission is carried out quickly and in its short lifetime, and it succeeds in bringing about helpful change that will be of benefit to all of mankind. This brave soul's brief incarnation touches many people and raises awareness and consciousness of the sanctity of life.

One of the best examples of a young life being cut tragically short as part of its soul's greater mission is the story of Nicholas Green that changed the entire planet. Here are his words of wisdom:

"Hi, my name is Nicholas Green. I was an organ donor because I got shot in Italy. I want everyone to listen to my daddy when he talks about the importance of donating organs. If my family could do it, so could you. Why waste perfectly good organs on a dead body? The body doesn't need them anymore and you could be like me and help seven people to get new parts that work.

"I like Canada, Daddy, and I wish you could see me there with you on your talk. Mom, I like my new sister and brother and want to tell Eleanor that I think she's a nice girl. Don't let her eat too many sweets, Mom, 'cos the cavities she's got will get worse.

"I take care of the animals up here and they don't bite like when they were alive. I like them and they like me. When I come back someday, I will be a scientist! I am learning lots of things, Mom and Daddy, and you would be proud of me. I am not as quiet as I used to be either. The angels make me laugh and take me for rides on their wings. It's neat! Jesus is real, Mom, just like you said! He's very nice, too.

"Don't cry for me, please. I'm not sad, why are you? I can see you and I watch you all of the time. I am with you but I am also here. That's kind of strange, I guess, but when you get here, you'll see what I mean. Martin will be louder than I was, but not as funny as me. I kiss Laura's head to stop her from fussing, Mom, so you can sleep. Her hair is so soft, softer than Martin's. I love all of you and like the pictures that Eleanor draws. I like her colors. I will talk to you again someday. Love you, Nicky."

Ariel interrupted my reverie by touching me lightly on the shoulder and saying, "Diana, I am needed elsewhere. Would you go on along with Raphael? I know that you are no longer afraid at our partings and I am very glad for it. You know that we will be reunited again."

She smiled and quickly disappeared. Ariel was right, I was no longer fearful at our separations. Instead, I looked forward to our reunions with anticipation. She and I were like old school chums who after a separation, chatted endlessly, sharing our different experiences and thoughts when once we were brought together again.

While I flew up to the level of healing with Raphael, I kept trying to look at him without calling attention to the fact. Well, I should have known better. As an archangel, he is extremely perceptive, intelligent, and most of all, knowing.

"Diana, I'm going to stop flying and stand here so you can get a good look at me!"

I suddenly had a new experience. For the first time since I arrived here, I was embarrassed! I had forgotten about that human emotion. Oh dear, I imagine my aura was bright red. I looked the other way entirely and could not meet his gaze at all.

"Diana, we are suspended in midair and are not going anywhere until you satisfy your curiosity." Raphael's voice came at me like deep rolling thunder through his laughter.

I felt so safe just to be near to him. He is the archangel of healing and, as I found out, quite the prankster. "It is often said, Diana, that I am the angel with a sense of humor."

Raphael's eyes twinkled in delight as he told me this. I had quite forgotten my earlier embarrassment and was now looking him full in the face. Of course, it is quite impossible to even know what an archangel *really* looks like, but I will describe how he appeared to me. His short, curly jet black hair framed his eyes which shone like precious jewels bathed in a soft blue light. His features were strong and kind and capped off quite nicely by his mouth which was always ready to smile and then to quickly laugh. Raphael's laugh was a hearty laugh that seemed to come from somewhere deep within him. This angel never held back.

His gown, the color of the azure sky on a balmy summer's day, trailed endlessly behind him and matched the color of his eyes exactly. His arms rippled with muscles and his hands were large and strong. I had held his powerful hand while flying with him yet had felt only tender gentleness emanating from it.

"Raphael, why were you chosen for healing purposes and, do the other angels have a sense of humor as well?" I asked of this majestic angel while quite boldly staring into his beautiful eyes. They calmed and soothed me so that I could communicate openly with him without any trace of my usual shyness.

"I was not chosen, but created. God knew what he was doing when he made me just as he knew what he was doing when he made you."

At the mention of God having made me, my shyness quickly returned. I smiled the tiniest bit and ducked my head down. I did not want to talk about me but about him. Raphael lifted my chin with his finger and brought my gaze back to his wonderful eyes.

"Precious child of God, you and I have the same spirit within us, do we not? We are both healers and we both use laughter as a bridge to others, as do all the angels. None is greater than the other—human or angel."

His tremendous healing love enveloped me as his wings fanned out, gathering me to him. "I give you the gift of peace, Diana."

A vibrant blue glow flared out from his wings and totally surrounded me. All at once, I was at peace, the most perfect, profound peace. I felt renewed, strengthened and oh, so blessed.

We continued on our way to the level of healing. As we alighted upon this place of healing, love and compassion, we were met by many of the angels who had tended me when I had previously been on this level. It was so good to be back amongst my dear angel friends once more. We merged our energies together into what you may call a group hug. So many feelings of love and laughter passed between us as we shared in our welcoming of one another. Raphael joined with us, casting his blue healing light upon the entire level.

As I came away from the group hug, I looked about the level and remembered that it had a yellow cast to it when I had been here before. The atmosphere was now a mix of yellow and blue, and I rather liked it better that way.

Zeil, the main angel who had ministered to me when I had been here before, explained. "Diana, this healing level is usually just yellow because it calms the newly-arrived souls and also the souls who are called back up here for additional healing. But, with Raphael's influence, blue has been added to aid the souls in their communications with you. Normally, we do not want the new souls to communicate, but to rest. We have asked Raphael to bring you here today to help us in our healings by bringing you together again with some of the patients you healed in your own way while you were alive."

I was touched and humbled to the depths of my soul that these extremely capable healing angels would request my assistance. The glow of their healing love so filled my heart and soul that I briefly wondered why I had thought to turn down their previous offer of letting me stay amongst them forever. But then I reminded myself that I knew in my heart that I had many other places to go, many more things to learn, and that I was not going to stay in heaven forever. Not just yet, anyway. I meant to keep the promise I had made to myself while I had been upon Pebble Island. I would take in every scrap of knowledge I could and use it within my next lifetime. I wanted so very much to live a lifetime of love and happiness.

Raphael interrupted my thoughts and told me to look to my right. Seated there were rows upon rows of souls I had met in the various hospitals I had visited while I had been alive. I did not recognize them by their looks but by their hearts. One after the other, they came forward to tell me how much my visiting had blessed their weakened spirits and had rekindled a hope within them that they were worthy of love, acceptance and respect.

The souls of those who suffered and died of AIDS asked that I speak for them to all of you. This is what they wanted me to tell you.

When people are told that they have AIDS, they know—at this point in time, anyway—that it is their death sentence. What they do *not* need to hear at this time is, "How did you get it?" Instead, they need to hear words such as, "I am here for you. I will not leave you nor will I judge you or be ashamed of you."

Upon hearing that it will be loved and cared for, the spirit will thrive, perhaps battle for life longer, and will not have quite as much pain. The spirit who hears only blame and accusation will give up quickly and die a lonely, pain-filled death. The spirits who, while they were still souls in heaven, agreed to reincarnate and contract AIDS did so to make people aware that everyone, no matter what their sexual preference, is first and foremost, a human being and has the right to be helped and cared for in their hour of greatest need.

The AIDS victims realize that every one of us must be responsible for our choices and decisions. However, that does not give society free license to be mean and aggressive towards those who may differ in anyway from its accepted standards. In fact, one of the greatest lessons for the rest of the population is to reveal the level of compassion for fellow human beings who are suffering.

Further, souls who have agreed to be afflicted with the AIDS virus are actually purging any karma they may have amassed throughout their various past lifetimes. The AIDS sufferer will go through public humiliation, self-loathing, terror and great physical pain. By choosing to go through this, they will have the opportunity to love and forgive themselves and others as their illness progresses. Their souls will speak quite clearly to them and will, if they are willing, lead them step-by-step to a greater understanding of who they are and what they came here to do.

If they listen to their souls before their deaths, they will have greater peace and love about them than they ever had before. The doctors, nurses, family and friends who are with them while in hospital will see this aura of love around them and also receive healing. They will know that their patient or loved one is at peace, and they themselves will have a greater understanding of the spirit of love. These doctors, nurses, family and friends will then go out into the world and demonstrate that spirit of love by removing the shame of AIDS through education and public awareness. We are not to shun anyone who has a disease, but are to give them our encouragement, love and support. As I have said before and will say again, the world's healing depends upon it.

When I had visited them in hospital, sitting on their beds, holding their hands, the AIDS patients told me that they had all been quite amazed that a princess would do such a thing, and even more astonishingly, that she was not afraid to do so.

I found their surprise at my lack of fear funny and I laughed. Then I would explain that I had talked with many doctors who had told me that a person cannot contract AIDS by holding a victim's hand or by sitting on his or her bed. In other words, I went on, knowledge is key. Lack of knowledge is ignorance that breeds fear and prejudice that only enables negativity to grow and multiply boundlessly.

So many of the souls gathered beside me told me of the honor I had paid to them by sitting with them, talking to them and, most importantly, listening to them. Many, many of them had no one to visit them and feared that they would die alone in hospital, totally unloved and unacknowledged. Through my visits with them, they received a healing and a blessing within their souls that uplifted and gladdened them so much so that they said they had then been able to die with dignity and not with shame.

Their praise and kind words once again touched me so that I quickly gathered all of my beautiful friends to me, and with the help of Raphael and the healing angels, we embraced in a spirited healing hug.

I then told them, "You, too, healed a part of me at a time in my life when I so needed love and acceptance. When I would revisit hospital and learn that one of you had passed since my last visit, I would say a special prayer just for you, wishing you Godspeed into the healing light of God and his angels."

Each soul upon this level will continue to receive the healing they need until they can once again contemplate reincarnating or going any further in their spiritual growth. They need the rest and truly deserve it.

Having learned that the soul invariably chooses the time and means of the death of every incarnation, I was curious as to why one would choose AIDS-related illnesses as their avenue of departure from the earthly realms, so I went to ask. Now, there are many healing levels where I am. For instance, I was put upon a healing level where angels attended to me while I was in a sleep-like state. Other spirits will go to their own unique levels such as large groups of spirits who perish together in plane crashes, wars, mass deaths as in earthquakes or such places as concentration camps, and spirits who had been afflicted with the AIDS virus. All are put on a level of healing with those who they shared the death experience with, or maybe one that was similar but at a different time.

Remember now, this is only for matters of healing; once initial healing is complete, the spirit then goes on without the group to other levels appropriate to that individual. When a group of people die together, there is a connectedness among them and the connection continues on the healing level. They go there immediately following death to heal not only as individuals, but as a group, as well.

I want to share with you what these souls have to say about why they chose to live a life in which they would be afflicted with AIDS, what they hoped to learn from it and what they wanted to teach others by virtue of their own suffering. Daniel will be the first to speak, then Patti.

"My name is, or was, Daniel. When I had been in spirit before this past life, my spirit guide informed me that I needed the experience of being the object of public disdain. I had never experienced that in any other lifetime I had lived and so it was about time I got this necessary learning experience over with. The means we selected to bring about this public disdain was by being gay and contracting the AIDS virus.

"Now when people say that being gay is a choice, they couldn't be more right, but it is a choice of the spirit, not the personality. The choices of gender and sexual preference are made before incarnating, while you are still in spirit, not once you are on the earth. I wanted to teach people compassion, sympathy, and to have an open mind and heart regarding those who are different.

"It proved harder than I thought, and I'm glad that this lifetime was short—I died at the age of 29. After experiencing what I did, I would never again put a double whammy on my soul like I did in this past lifetime. First, being gay is hard enough, but then to compound matters by allowing myself to contract AIDS was nothing short of lunacy.

"If you detect a note of anger, resentment and extreme remorse in my words, you are absolutely correct. I have been on this level since March, 1996 in earth time, and am just now working through all of what I had put upon myself. There is also a lot of self-pity remaining which, of course, hinders my healing. I have made progress in some areas but I just can't seem to get past the anger around my spirit guide knowing what I was in for and not letting me know fully what I was about to do.

"I am the type of spirit who needs abundant love and acceptance. I found that being extremely different was not the way to get the acceptance I needed for who I am. My guide tells me that after a little more healing, I will be put upon the level of forgiveness so that I can begin working on forgiving myself. Actually, I think I need to forgive my guide, too.

"Ah, but you know, one thing remains—I have learned many, many truths while I have been here, the most important one being that in spirit as in life, we are all ultimately responsible for our decisions and our actions. There! I said it! You, dear readers, have just witnessed me taking a giant leap in my own healing. The group is now cheering, for they, too, have healed a bit because I have.

"I will not recount the ordeal of the public disdain nor the pain I endured through being rejected by my family. No matter how much I tried while alive, I could not bridge the gap between us. I do not wish to relive the agony of it all in my soul's memory.

"During the months after my death, my family talked with many people about what it is like to be an isolated gay who is also an AIDS victim. Their grief opened their hearts. So I will say, therefore, that my family and community learned that I was not a monster who needed to be hidden away from society. I have forgiven my family for turning their backs on me after I told them I had AIDS, but they need to forgive themselves as well. They had sent me away to live out the remainder of my days without knowing or caring whether I was receiving any aid or care. Upon hearing of my death through my lover, my family came together and grieved for me and for what we had put each other through. So, the teaching that I was to do I did through my death."

"My name is Patti and I was a nurse. I contracted AIDS in 1983 by getting stuck with a needle I had used to inject an AIDS patient. I passed away in 1990. I lived in Albuquerque, NM, and just loved it. I loved my life, I loved my work.

"First, in case you are wondering about Ryan White, the boy who contracted AIDS through blood transfusions, Ryan was one of the first pioneers of AIDS. He opened our eyes to the fact that AIDS was not just a gay man's disease. Ryan has left this healing level and is now upon a level of learning to prepare for his next incarnation.

"Why did I set this up for myself? Because I knew at the soul level that I needed to learn compassion, and how better to learn than to experience for myself what it would be like to have a hated, fearful disease such as AIDS.

"Once it was discovered that I had AIDS, I had to quit my job. I was married and had two children, but my husband earned a decent living and could support us adequately, at least for a time. Once my illness got to the point where I was bedridden, I was put into a state-run nursing home. My husband's insurance did not cover AIDS and its related illnesses, and we knew that we couldn't afford the cost of hospitalization.

"While most of the nurses and orderlies were very nice to me, some refused to even come into my room for fear that I might contaminate them. In the 1980s, not as much was known about AIDS as it is today, but nonetheless it broke my heart to be whispered about and to be thought of as a person to be avoided at all costs.

"I was not being treated for my AIDS other than just being made as comfortable as possible and so I slept most of the last two years of my life away. I am not sorry that I chose this for myself, in fact, with my consent, my husband donated my body to science for research, and I hope that, because of my life and death, many more will be helped and possibly cured..

"I know that my time on this healing level is coming to an end, but before I leave this group of dearly loved souls, I want to make sure that I do everything within my personal power to help the group understand something very important—that through our lives and deaths, all of us here provided an opportunity for all of mankind to grow. And, that's really what it's all about."

As my beloved Raphael and I left the level of healing, I looked back once more to wave and to project the thought to them that we would be reunited again. As I did so, I noticed that the lighting on that level had returned to its former light yellow glow. This is as it should be, I thought. The dear souls upon it are weary and very much in need of rest.

There truly is a time for everything in heaven as well as on earth. I smiled merrily as I thought of all the good times I will share with my dearly loved former patients once they are fully healed. I turned to look at Raphael and joined him in a joyful laugh as we soared ever higher into the heavens. I knew that he was taking me onto my next level of learning, but, for now, I savored this most precious time of spirited flying through the cosmos with the very mighty and beautiful archangel Raphael.

Chapter 8

Fellow Travelers

RAPHAEL DROPPED ME OFF ON A LEVEL WITH MANY LARGE MAN-sion-like buildings on it, some as grand as the great castles of the world, only these were even more magnificent.

"Why are you not coming along with me?" I asked.

"I have much to do on the earth plane with my work of healing and bringing light and laughter into the lives of those who are hurting in any way."

"Well, just what is it I'm to do exactly?" I inquired.

"Go find out, Diana, and have a good time doing it," he replied as he disappeared from my view.

I abhor it when my questions are not answered and I am left to my own wits. I felt angry and abandoned. Why was I still feeling so many human feelings? Why wasn't I always at perfect peace up here? Isn't that what heaven is about—perfect peace? I had no intentions of going knocking about, troubling the residents of this level. Just what would I say to these souls anyway?

I turned my back on the mansions and walked down a path that led into a field of wildflowers, kicking as many pebbles and stones as I could along the way. When I entered the field, I was soothed quite a bit by the many different lovely flowers and astonished by their tremendous beauty. I had never seen flowers such as these, the colors of each and every flower shot up from it and glowed like neon into the air.

"Diana, do you see how the flowers reflect the essence of their natures out into the universe?" a voice asked.

I had not sensed anyone near and quickly whirled around to see who had spoken to me. I saw a figure robed in white leaning against a tree. My spirit soared and leaped for joy within me! Without having to be introduced, I knew who it was in an instant— Jesus Christ!

I was struck dumb at the sight of his magnificence. Waves of love, gentleness and mercy radiated from him. I could not move, for if I could have, I would have fainted dead away.

He held out his hand to me and laughingly said, "Diana, come to me. You will not faint, I promise you."

I walked or rather glided, really, over to Jesus. I reached out to take his hand and as I did so, I looked closely at it. Just as in any drawing or painting I have ever seen of him, his hand had a mark on it, as if something had gone through the middle of his palm.

"Jesus, is this truly from a nail?" I could barely hold the thought without sobbing.

"Yes, but I do not feel the pain of the nail any longer."

He kissed my hand as I held onto his and he added, "Do not cry for me, Diana, I did the will of my father as you have done also. You, too, bear the mark of a nail."

I looked quickly at my own hand and was totally bewildered and confused for there was not a mark upon it, let alone one from a nail.

Before I could ask him what he meant, Jesus replied, "All of my father's children who do his will happily and joyfully bear the mark of the nails that pierced my skin. Who among you has not been battered and bruised by others and had your kindness rebuked and thrown back into your face? Have you not been ridiculed for your good works and also been told to stop?"

Jesus did not need me to confirm his questions. I remembered well the many times that the men in gray had told me, "Stop making a ridiculous spectacle of yourself by showing off and pretending that you are someone important. The only reason anyone pays you any mind at all is because you are married to the prince and have borne the royal heir. Your public works mean nothing to anyone and you are making such a slight difference that no one would notice if you simply stopped."

As this painful memory surfaced, I realized just how much their words had hurt me at the time. Jesus brought me to him and I sobbed greatly into his chest as he hugged my pain away. I had thought that I was over all of my previous life's anguish, but found that not to be true.

Over my wrenching sobs, I heard him say, "You did well, Diana. You carried the love of God within you and helped and healed many people. Without this love, you would not have had it in your heart to aid anyone at all. I want you to know that it was God who strengthened you and loved you through the hardest times of your life. It was he who brought the people into your life that helped and healed you so that you could continue on in your work."

"But, Jesus, who helped and healed me?"

He did not answer immediately but took me by the hand through the field of flowers that seemed to go on forever. I wondered where he was taking me. I saw a bench ahead and welcomed the idea of sitting down with Jesus. I was not tired; the only time I had felt tired was when I had first arrived on the healing level. I wanted to sit with Jesus just for the experience of it. I wanted to lean against him and draw upon his strength, comfort and great love.

Without uttering a thought to me, Jesus showed me in images who had helped and healed me. It was as if my mind were a screen and he the projectionist. He showed me pictures of my favorite times with my boys, and I watched as I held each one as a newborn. I witnessed again their first tentative steps and smiled as I saw myself tucking them into bed, hugging them, kissing them and feeling their love return to me tenfold.

Next upon my mind's screen was Sarah Ferguson. I felt again the rush of relief that her friendship brought into my life, the "us against them" camaraderie that was the hallmark of our togetherness and the glue that bound us together in the beginning.

Jesus projected many more faces of the people that I had known while alive and seen while I had been on the Level of Mirrors. All of them had come into my life at a time when I desperately needed confirmation, attention and love.

"Diana, all of these people, both for better and worse, have helped you to grow in so many ways. When someone in your life prickles at you and makes you uncomfortable, do not think that they are not sent from God as well as the ones who bring you comfort and joy. God uses everybody in your life to guide, to teach, to help and to heal you. Do you understand?"

I nodded that I did.

"Some had a direct lesson to teach you and some had an indirect lesson. It seems you had the greatest problem with the ones who came to teach you indirectly."

I gave Jesus a quizzical look and he explained, "The people who were bothersome and irksome to you had been that way in order to teach you patience and to show you your own limits. As you grew to know yourself better, you found that you did not have to be hostile or devious to be rid of them. Instead, you eventually chose to release them in your mind and heart and they bothered you no more."

Jesus smiled at me a smile that told me I had done the right thing. I had slowly grown to listen to my heart instead of my head and had been successful far more often than I had previously given myself credit for. I thought back to the many times I had fired innocent workers from my staff because I had been in a bad mood or had assumed, in my tormented state at the time, that they sided with Charles rather than with me. I see now that I had let my imagination think for me instead of my logic. I should have talked to someone I trusted back then and aired my feelings through them before jumping to conclusions that resulted in a staff member becoming unemployed. I apologize most humbly to anyone who had been in my employ that I had wrongfully discharged.

Jesus took both of my hands into his own and said, "You are forgiven, Diana."

I looked up into his face and melted into his eyes, kind yet full of great strength. His reddish brown hair was not as long as the paintings of him depict but instead was a very flattering length, just to his ears and pushed back from his face. It was wavy and very shiny. It looked very soft and I wanted to touch it.

"You may," he said, of course reading my thought as if I had spoken it. And so I did. I was right, his hair was very soft. The thought then went through my mind that he didn't have a look about him that I could pinpoint as to what his race would be.

He answered my thought with another. "I am every race. I am every denomination. I am every man, woman and child. What I am cannot be split or divided. I am one with all, and in all. I am love. I am."

How I love him so. I cannot explain the love I have for Jesus; it is deep within my soul and is everlasting as he is everlasting.

Jesus then explained to me that what we project on the outside comes from the inside but is not all-inclusive of what we are soul-deep. I, for example, took the posture of one who was shy. I am not shy on the inside, but projected shyness as a way of defense towards others hurting me. After all, who would purposely hurt a shy person?

"You do not need that defense," he told me.

In that moment, I realized that what you feel on the inside you should project to others. If you have any fears about how others will perceive you, pray before going out that you will be received as a person of the light, that any negativity surrounding you will be deflected into the love and light of God and will not harm you. Pray that you will perceive others as beloved souls of the light as well. Guard your heart through prayer, not your imagination.

I replied, "Like you, I should be totally open and yet totally protected, but without falsehood. Oh, I have so many questions to ask of you."

"Go ahead, Diana, ask me what you wish."

"First, why is there so much confusion about religions? Which is the true religion?"

"There is confusion because people make it confusing. Those who have love in their hearts have God also. God is not the sole property of one religion or theology. His great wisdom and love abounds for all. Those who seek him shall find him. He is within.

"True religion? What is religion? It is man's written and verbal communication representing God and, as such, is misrepresented by manmade doctrine. Many writings from every denomination and religion say that God is love and understanding, and that he wants his children to seek and to love him with their hearts, minds, bodies and souls. That is the truth of God. It angers me when people put more into their religious books than was originally intended. More people are lost to God through manmade theology than through anything else. God is universal."

"Thank you. Are you God?" I asked next.

"I am. I am also God's son and his holy spirit. The true form of God is too powerful and beyond human comprehension to appear as he truly is. God is pure light. He is a blazing light that cannot be seen until there is nothing in the way of you and this perfect light. That is the reason for many incarnations. Through living many times, you become more perfect. Until you reach total perfection, you may not look upon God."

"Then why does God let evil exist within the world?"

"What is evil, Diana? Is it when an innocent person gets hurt or murdered? Is it when a great disaster comes about through nature? What is evil to some may be of benefit to others. When people lose their jobs, for instance, they think that perhaps something evil has befallen them instead of looking at it as a chance to start over, to start something better, something greater. No, they look at it as an unhappy event within their lives. Think about the person who will be hired to replace the worker who was let go. Perhaps that person needed the position even more than the other one did. Now, if you knew that, you would, of course, look at this evil happening in a totally differently light, wouldn't you?

"As for those who lose their lives through murder, disease or natural disaster, every soul will and must experience these things within many lifetimes. It is also through these things that improvements come to the human race. People become more aware of their connection to one another when a fellow human being's life is taken through violence or a tragedy of some sort.

"So many souls willingly give up their lives so that change will be effected for the betterment of all. It is not always apparent immediately, but if you look back over the annals of history, you would see that many laws and other changes have been made because of the one who lost his or her life so that other lives will be spared.

"Not all of the souls upon the earth seek God. Some seek to bring about death and despair. These souls have free will as much as godly souls do. God will not interfere with the will of man until it is time for him to do so. The time will come when there will be no more war, disease or death. But it is in God's time and no other. Remember that souls agree to what they will experience within their lives and that everyone within that life plays a part, both the godly and the ungodly. God comforts those who lose loved ones and will heal their hearts and minds with love, peace and understanding."

Then Jesus stood and held out his hand to me. "Come with me."

I touched his hand and knew that it was time to move on to a place where further answers would be given. In an instant, we were back at the beginning of the path of flowers. Touched by heaven's sunlight, the beautiful mansions gleamed brightly as countless angels flew around and about, sprinkling golden splashes of color onto the roofs of the majestic homes. I did not ask why they were doing this but, instead, allowed myself simply to enjoy the pure beauty as I gazed on it.

"Diana, there is someone whom you should meet. He lived and died at the time of your own life and death. There is much the two of you can share about your experiences while alive in the flesh and while in spirit, too. Do you wish to meet him?"

I wanted very much to meet up with this person who had lived and died during my lifetime. I tried to read through Jesus' thoughts in order to learn whom he could be referring to but to no avail. He pointed down the lane and as I looked, I could make out a figure of someone coming towards us. The figure appeared to be gliding at a fast clip as if he had urgent business to attend to. Once he was clearly within my spiritual sight, I saw immediately who it was— Chris Farley. We both smiled from ear to ear. Jesus joined us as our spirits melded into one another and rejoiced together in total happiness and recognition.

"Diana, you helped me so much before when I was a new arrival. I just want to thank you and ask what it is that I can do for you. How can I help you?"

Chris was referring to his own Level of Mirrors when I had been requested by his spirit guide to walk him through the paces. I don't know time any longer, and it seemed to have been both very recently, and yet so long ago. Whenever it had been, it was fun being with him again.

Jesus looked straight into my heart and said, "Diana, I will leave you now. There are other souls who wish to converse with you, too. Listen to them with a heart of love, and understanding will be yours. I leave my peace with you."

Thousands of angels suddenly filled the heavenly skies. They hovered around and above Jesus, waiting to go onwards with him. They looked at him tenderly, adoringly and with much love. Their only wish? To be with him and to do his will.

"Thank you, Lord, for blessing me with your love and wisdom. I will do as you ask and listen with my heart to any and all who speak to me."

I felt a rush of gratitude and love for God, who loved me so much that he had sent his son, Jesus, to speak to me. Chris and I watched as the angels, awash with the colors of the rainbow, melded into Jesus' spirit and were gone.

"Wow, pretty cool huh, Diana?"

Turning to look at Chris, I just nodded my head in agreement. I didn't want to let go of this moment just yet. I wanted to savor and replay within my soul's memory this holy time that I had just had with Jesus, and so I chose not to project a single thought.

"Yeah, I know what you mean, Diana. It was pretty awesome when he came and talked with me and John, too."

Chris had been on his own island of aloneness at that time and had received a special gift of two visitors: Jesus and John Candy. His experience differed somewhat from mine, but he, too, talked with Jesus and was further gifted by being permitted to chat with a fellow comedian and actor friend.

At my suggestion, Chris Farley had also contacted Christine Toomey shortly after his death and has his own story to impart. It is funnier than mine, but I know that his story and mine, being different, yet at the same time so much the same, will help and guide those who read it.

Well, I could see that there was no getting around it. Chris Farley was here to talk with me, and talk we would. I knew that I had time in abundance to go over and over within my thoughts my time with Jesus. I knew that I would also see my beloved Jesus again.

"Diana, what did you think of when you first crossed over?"

"Well, I thought all kinds of things. At first, I was glad and filled with relief to be out of pain and to be surrounded by such amazing beauty. But after the initial joy came a let-down."

Chris interrupted, "Boy, you're lucky. I wasn't filled with joy at all, not for a long time. I didn't want to die and fought it with everything in me, even after I had been in heaven for a while."

"Chris, I didn't want to die either. However, I gladly accepted death over the immense physical pain that I was in. It was far too much for me to bear."

"Yeah, that makes sense. Why did you feel a let down though if you were so happy to be here?"

With his brow furrowed and his mouth set in a slight frown, I just had to smile, then laugh out loud. He had retained so much of his delightful boyishness that I felt a sudden burst of delight towards him and grabbed him up, hugging me to him.

This obviously startled him a bit and he said, "Whoa, hey, what did I do so I'll know to do it again?" he asked, laughing.

"You did nothing other than being just who you are. Chris, you are a delight to me and I love you for it. Now, as to why I felt a letdown, when I first came to heaven, I had been exiled on what I called Pebble Island. It was a place of aloneness and reminded me of my worst fear—being alone. My first reaction was to fight against it, just as you fought against your death. After a while, however, I accepted that I had to be alone in order to work through my issues and resolve them within my spirit. Then the happy day came that I could move onwards and upwards, so to speak."

Chris plunked down upon the ground and patted the spot next to him for me to do likewise. As I sat with him, I saw more spirits coming towards us. "Chris, do you know who these spirits are?" I asked.

"No, I don't, can't see 'em clearly yet. Hey, I wonder if they live in these mansions behind us."

As they approached, I pushed back a lock of Chris' blond hair from his forehead and asked him, "Do you understand your life and death better now?"

He answered, "Yeah, I do. It took me a while though, and I had to go through some pretty intensive training to get to this point, but it's been worth it."

He smiled, put his arm around my shoulders and added, "I'm glad we're buds, Diana. Who woulda thought it? Me and the princess. Wow!"

I laughed and grabbed a handful of grass, tossing it at his hair while I told him, "You are such a clown, Chris Farley. Half the time, I don't know if you're pulling my leg or not."

"I couldn't be more serious, Diana, and by the way, where *are* your legs?"

We both cracked up at that one. "Well, as my guide, Ariel, once told me, just because you can't see something doesn't mean it doesn't exist."

"Yeah, I know what she means. I feel my body, but when I look, there's hardly anything there. It's weird, man."

As the band of souls grew nearer, I could now see that there were some spirits I recognized and some I did not. It didn't matter to Chris or to myself if we knew them or not, for most were filled with a tremendous light that neither of us had seen before in a human spirit.

In response to our unspoken thoughts, we were told, "We are perfected spirits. We have evolved throughout many lifetimes and now reside permanently upon the heavenly plane. The spirit of God resides fully and completely within us and ours likewise within his.

"Oh man, how many lifetimes does it take to do something like that?" Chris asked, to no one in particular.

Blazing with the most glorious, multi-hued light, Mother Teresa stepped forward and answered, "Dear, Chris and Diana, it takes as many lifetimes as you wish to live through in order to arrive at completion. You see, it is up to your spirit and your soul to have an understanding or agreement. The two must become one in harmony and love, jointly agreeing that the goal is to live eternally with the creator. Once your soul and your spirit have experienced everything that they desire and need to in order to learn and to grow, you will have arrived at your completion."

Another brightly-glowing soul stepped forward, this one not recognizable as a worldly figure. "My name is Timus. I last lived a hundred years ago in Edinburgh, Scotland. The point of my coming to the two of you is to tell you that you both have earthly lives yet to live, and in order to live those lives fully and enjoyably, you must come to an agreement within your spirit and soul. Decide what it is that both spirit and soul need and then go about setting up your next life to accommodate the individual needs and desires of both your spirit and soul.

"The ideal would be to strike a balance, creating energies that your soul will learn and grow from, as well as creating energies that your spirit will learn and grow from. It is not impossible to do, however; I lived one too many times in misery until I finally listened to what completed souls here were trying to convey to me each time I was once again in spirit."

Timus faded into the background as Ariel stepped forward. "Chris and Diana, the souls that are gathered here with you have all been through what you yourselves are going through now. Mother Teresa was not a saint while she lived and yet most people would classify her as one. It is because she lived her life with both her heart and soul, and gave to both. She studied and learned before incarnating this last time and, as both of you now know, doing so served her well. Her spirit needed to be needed and her soul needed to touch the lives of the poor through her ministry of love and service to others.

"Looking at her earthly life, one may wonder why she would have wanted to live amongst the poorest of the poor and the diseased. This was the life lesson that Mother Teresa needed and desired, and so it was. She now has no other lives to complete and resides here in one of the beautiful mansions behind you where she serves God and humanity from her home. She directs her spiritual energies without ever leaving heaven."

Ariel stopped speaking and looked intently at us. I returned her gaze, telling her in my thoughts that there was much left for me to learn yet and that I was far from ready to reincarnate. She smiled and lightly touched the top of my head, saying, "Yes, you have much to learn, Diana, but your heart is filled with love and compassion. You will travel much more quickly to inner wisdom than you realize."

"And what about me?" Chris Farley asked, looking to Ariel for an answer.

"Chris, you too have much love inside." She lightly touched the top of his head as well and added, "Your spirit guide will continue to lead you well. Please listen to him in the spirit of cooperation, dear heart. Your guide is your friend as well as your teacher."

Smiling, Ariel beckoned another spirit to step forward. This spirit was not filled with the light as the other spirits had been and I knew instantly that it was someone who would reincarnate very soon.

"Yes, Diana, you're right. I go to the level of the scribes after I say what I need to here. It is my hope that this next lifetime will be my last. That being so, I would like to say to both of you that to find inner cooperation, you must examine your spirit and soul separately. Let them each have a voice and a turn.

"Sometimes, as in my case, the spirit overwhelms the quietness of my soul and drowns it out, so that the spirit does not even realize that it is not listening to the soul. I needed to learn how to quiet my spirit and believe I've learned how to do so. I was a male in my most recent past incarnation, and now I will go back as a female. I am going to live a life in which I know I will face all the past unresolved problems that I did not deal with successfully during a previous lifetime.

"I will once again incarnate into a wealthy family in the San Francisco Bay area, which was also home to me during my last incarnation. In my previous lifetime during the 1930s, I was an alcoholic with manic depression. Little was known of either disease at that time, so naturally, I was never treated. I literally wasted my parents' patience and money and never did anything constructive with my life. I wanted to be a writer in the worst way but could not get my spirit to quiet within me.

"While I have been here, I have learned the reason for this. When a soul incarnates and chooses the burden of alcohol and mental disease, the spirit within the person is not affected by the diseases but talks constantly to the ego and the soul, demanding that something be done for the physical body that contains it. I have learned that our spirits care very much for our physical, emotional and mental well-being because it is the spirit's desire to complete the tasks that have been chosen for the lifetime and it knows that those tasks will not be accomplished if the person is left to their troubles without any help or aid.

"I had chosen to be afflicted with these diseases with the intent of meeting the challenge of rising above them. When I, at the spirit level, made this choice, I did not know that manic depressives often struggle violently against the very things that will help them. Also, they compulsively cling to the very things, such as alcohol, that will keep them in the grip of the disease. After I had passed from that lifetime, I asked my spirit guide, 'Why didn't you tell me beforehand that I'd picked an almost impossible combination of burdens to overcome?'

"My guide informed me, 'You needed to experience that lifetime for various reasons. First, you learned through that life to be compassionate towards those with afflictions. Second, you learned how not to be an enabler as your mother had been for you. You recall how she would try to pick you up out of your depressive moods by giving you money, cars, vacations and anything else she could think of that might coax you out of your bad humor, as she called it.'

"He was right, of course. No life, even a dissolute one, is wasted from the soul perspective. In the end, I was thankfully removed from that painful life at age 25 when I wrapped myself around a tree, ironically in a car my mother bought me—a 1937 Ford Coupe.

"After many levels of healing and learning, I am now ready to face another lifetime. I want to give to my family and to society this time by way of incarnating as a female who I feel certain will be able to overcome the same family challenges that I had faced previously and will go on to become a doctor or nurse who works with alcoholic manic depressives. Wish me well, and may you both live well."

Billions of souls are constantly coming and going throughout the heavenly and earthly realms in order to eventually achieve completion. There are, of course, many souls upon the level of completion; however it takes many, many lifetimes before a soul is made perfect. Amongst the crowd of spirits, I caught sight of many who had lived during Chris' and my last lifetime. Ariel said they had gathered here with their guides in order to hear what the completed souls had to say.

Some souls within the crowd had lived only one or two lives thus far, whereas some older souls had lived 150 lives or more. One particularly old soul stepped out of the crowd and came towards us—John Lennon. I mention him by name because I know that many people will relate to him and will be more willing to learn because of how much he meant to so many while he was alive. This is no way detracts from the other souls who were not as well known while alive. Their stories are just as important and just as valid.

John came over to us and plopped down on the ground. "Hello, Diana. How are you doing, Chris?" He was friendly and quite eager to start talking to us. After we greeted one another, John started in straight away, "I've noticed some changes in spiritual consciousness on the earth since I've last been there but, man, they still have so much further to go."

Chris added, "Boy, you got that right!"

With a very straight face, John asked him, "Chris, have you noticed the polar complexities of the socioeconomic group you recently departed?"

Chris looked at John with a put-on confused expression for a moment, then immediately launched into a reply in a very British accent which is not easy when you are just using thought telepathy. Sounding like a BBC announcer, Chris said, "Yes, I have, John, and I find therein lies the problem. You see, money and class play a large role in how most people perceive the importance or lack thereof of their own self-worth. Too much money and the person may suffer from an inflated ego and may entertain fears that others love them for their social standing and their money alone. Not enough money and the individual may suffer from low self-esteem and seriously doubt their ability to attract friends and a mate."

Chris sat back, smiled a lopsided grin at John and raised an eyebrow at him as he waited for John's reply. We were all quite amused and delighted at how Chris used his wonderful humor to bring John up short. It was all done in good sport and John laughed the longest and the hardest, knowing that he had tried only moments earlier to make jest of Chris.

"Farley, you really need to reincarnate, man. The world sorely needs your humor. You really had me going there for a moment with your poor rendition of a Brit. I thought at first that I had you."

We all chuckled once more and then settled down to listen to John. "As I've traveled all over this and many other levels, I've found the only truth to be that humans need more love and understanding. No one can give love if they first do not possess it within. Everyone on every level here knows that, but how do we hold on to the knowledge long enough and firmly enough once we reincarnate?

"Every prophet and enlightened being has spouted that mankind needs love within in order to demonstrate it. So, it's my theory that there's just no way around it. All of us will have to live again and again and go through needless pain and suffering until we wake up and smell the truth, the truth being that all are created equal. Equal in that we all need love and acceptance. But first, it starts with self-acceptance and self-love, and without that, no one will move too far ahead in the game of life. And life really is a game, isn't it? The winners are those who surrender to their spiritual truths. The losers are those who are too afraid to look at their own spirituality because they might see their lack and feel their emptiness and know that they have short-changed themselves. They've let go of their spirit connection and therefore let go of their true selves. The life they lead on earth is a shallow, hollow existence of empty days and empty nights."

Another spirit stepped forward just then and said, "I've lived many lifetimes and never found happiness while alive. I've been wealthy, poor, strong and weak. But no matter what, I never found my true spirit in any of those lives. John, with what you've seen in your learning, what do you suggest I can do to live a successful life?"

John tilted his head skyward for an instant then looked back at the soul in front of him. He took the spirit's hands into his own and said, "You say that you've lived many lifetimes?"

"Yes."

"Hmmm ... I know that this can't be the first time you've been on this level, so I ask you, what is your definition of a successful life?"

The spirit answered without hesitation, "To be a good person."

John let go of the spirit's hands and quickly turned towards the large crowd gathered in front of us. "There, you see? Did you all hear this dear misguided soul?"

A few spirits slowly nodded their heads. It was very much apparent to me, however, that many of the others still did not understand. John jumped up and spoke excitedly to the crowd, "Don't you get it yet? Our lives on earth are not about being good people! Life on earth is about being the best that we can be within the context of our spirituality, not about being good, or bright, or popular or anything like that. That stuff just doesn't last, but your soul does! The answer is to start living as if the enrichment of your soul depended upon it, because believe me, it does! Your soul has got to be the most important thing to you, not the things that your ego needs."

John flopped back down upon the ground and smiled up at everyone. "Okay, that's the truth according to John Lennon. Take it or leave it. But if you're willing, try my truth in your next lifetime and see what happens, I think you'll be pleasantly surprised."

As John merged back into the crowd, Chris told me that he could hear his guide calling him and that he must go. I thanked him for coming to me to compare notes and hugged him once again, absorbing his love and laughter as I did.

"Diana, I want to reincarnate with you and marry you," Chris said, quite seriously.

"When I am ready to reincarnate, I will check with you first and perhaps we will be able to have a soul agreement between the two of us."

He whooped for joy and leapt into the air. "Good-bye for now, Diana. I'll talk with you again way before you even consider reincarnating. Okay?"

"Okay, Chris, go with my love." With that, he faded from my view.

When I looked once again in the direction of the assembled souls, they were no longer there. "Where did they go, Ariel?"

"They came to say what they needed to say and now are once again going about their various duties. You are free to go to any level you wish in order to learn and grow further."

I immediately thought of the Level of Healing and my dolphin friends. I had so much to contemplate, and I wanted to do so on a level that I knew would help me to absorb everything that was needed by both my spirit and my soul. Besides, my inner child was telling me quite excitedly that she needed to tell me a thing or two about how to have a happy childhood and how to pick the best parents in order to achieve this. I couldn't wait to hear what she had to say.

Away I went with my guide towards my most beloved of levels—the level of healing—and, as quick as a flash, I was with my dolphin friends. I was overjoyed to see them and they were delighted to see me, as well. I swam about with them for a very long time—at least what I imagine what a long time is since we do not measure time here.

They took me to the depths of the ocean and showed me beautifully colored fish that spoke quite clearly to me, chattering on and on about how wonderful their lives were and about how happy they were to be free of the cares they'd had while they lived within the earth's oceans. I had never thought before that fish might have worries and cares, and it struck me as extremely funny. I had to work hard at suppressing my thoughts of laughter lest the dear little fish thought that I was making jest of them.

The dolphins and I have made fast friends with one another, but there is a particular dolphin named Aphene (a-*fee*-nee) with whom I have formed a very close attachment. Aphene told me that my inner child was waiting for me on the shore and that I should go to her now.

Suddenly I was on the shore without having had to swim back towards it, and I took my inner child into my arms immediately. I was initially a bit surprised that she could come and go in and out of me at her will.

Little Diana answered my confusion, "Inner children have a will apart from that of their adult self. Our main purpose is to connect with the adult versions of ourselves, but we sometimes go wandering about while the adult is otherwise occupied."

I found this rather fascinating and quite extraordinary. "How can an inner child be so very much a part of our existence without us ever being aware of it?" I asked.

Little Diana said, "Because you, the adult, choose not to listen."

In my defense, I protested, "Well, I for one did not ever hear the smaller version of myself asking to be heard."

"But you did. You just thought that you were being immature and acting like a child when you heard my voice. You took it to be your adult voice, but it wasn't."

"I'm sorry, I don't understand. You're saying that you were trying to talk to me while I was alive and I dismissed it as my own immaturity?"

"When you needed comforting, you would wrap yourself in a giant quilt and sometimes feel 'babyish.' That was me telling you that I needed to be held close and to be kept warm. When you ate for comfort, that was me telling you that I just needed a treat, but then you would make yourself throw up and I was punished, too."

"Oh, I see what you mean. Well, I am very sorry. I had no idea that I was giving to you and at the same time taking away by undoing my comforting actions. I am so very, very sorry."

My inner child gently took me by the hand and we walked along the shore. "Diana, I want to tell you how you can assure yourself of having a childhood and parents better suited for you for your next lifetime."

I was all ears and told her, "Speak directly to my heart and mind so that what you tell me will stick with me when it comes time for me to choose the people to be in my next lifetime."

"When you know your inner child, you know yourself. Think about what it is that I need by thinking back over what it was that you denied yourself consistently during your past lifetime."

I thought for a moment and said, "Well, let's see. From when I was a very young girl, I denied myself the right to be who I was. Instead, to make everyone happy and keep things peaceful, I tried to be what they all wanted me be."

My inner child answered me quite concisely, hitting the nail on the head, "Right, but inside, you were miserable and at war with yourself all of the time."

I went on, "I wanted to be free of the constraints of my position within society. I did not want to put on airs and be a figurehead. At first, I'd wanted to be a ballerina and than found I was too tall for that. So then I thought that perhaps I would be happiest working with children and raising a family of my own."

"Yes, Diana, you did, but what you are forgetting is that when you were in spirit before, you had agreed to become the Princess of Wales and to go through everything that you did. However, you still could have honored your inner child and your adult self by listening a bit more carefully to what your spirit was telling you. It was trying to tell you that you were out of touch with not only your spirit but with your inner child, as well."

She paused to let that sink in and then continued, "Listening to your spirit would have told you that you picked this life for a reason and that you did not have to put on airs or be just a figurehead, but that you could combine your royal duties along with any personal desires you had regarding working with children. Listening to your inner child would have told you that that would have been more acceptable than wrapping yourself in a quilt or eating a meal. Do you see what I mean?"

"Yes, I do," I replied defensively, "but I want it to be understood that even as a child, I did not like the fact that certain behaviors were expected of me because of the family I was born into."

"Diana, as a child, you had no way of understanding why you were put here, but as an adult, you could have used more of the intuitive ability you possessed to reach deep into your soul for your answers."

"I see what you mean, and as far as choosing wisely the parents and situations of my next lifetime, you are suggesting that

I remember all that I experienced and learned within this past lifetime and then reflect on what it was that you needed from me?"

"Yes," she answered simply.

"But, how will that help me to choose better for myself concerning my next lifetime?"

My inner child looked up at me, smiled, and explained, "Because you will have the same needs and desires that you have always had since God made you. You need to be loved and cherished like everyone else. So, why not allow yourself the experience of being born into a family that will be more united in love than the other families you have chosen in the past?"

When she said that, I stopped walking and looked down into her eyes. In that moment, I learned one of the most profound truths imaginable. "Are you saying that I, or anyone else for that matter, can see the road ahead of them for their future lifetimes and arrange things in order to ease the journey along that road, and take on only those burdens that are absolutely necessary?"

"You got it!" My inner child giggled at my new found knowledge and smiled up at me most proudly.

"So, in other words, some of the burdens we take upon ourselves are totally unnecessary?"

Little Diana smiled and nodded her head vigorously.

"Oh dear! I see much more clearly now, but I wonder why I overburdened myself in each lifetime I've lived."

"Because you didn't listen to your spirit even when you *were* a spirit!"

At that profound insight, I grabbed little Diana up and held her close. "I give you my solemn pledge that from now on, I will only put myself through what is absolutely necessary for the purposes of a particular lifetime's growth. Thank you for teaching me that valuable soul lesson."

"Okay. *Now* can we play?"

Little Diana and I both longed to immerse ourselves in the living, healing waters of the sea, and so we linked arms and ran straight out to play with the waiting dolphins.

After a while, Ariel came to me to tell me something she knew I would want to hear, for she knew that in my heart I still treasured my association with Dodi Fayed and hoped to be instrumental in his healing. "Dodi is no longer on the forgiveness level."

I immediately sat down on the sand with her. "Thank you for coming to me with this news."

"Dodi has gone to the level of Rainbows. That's the level that teaches of learning to hope again. It will help him to see that even though he did not fulfill every life challenge that he had thought he might while alive, neither did he fail. The level of Rainbows teaches that even though spirits may strive during an incarnation to accomplish what they set out to, they do not always succeed. Hope is a very real thing, Diana, and it must be encouraged even here in the spirit realm, because Dodi, like you, will incarnate again and therefore, hope must be a part of his soul."

"But, Ariel, isn't hope just like crossing your fingers and wishing for the best? I thought that we created challenges that must be met? If those challenges are not met while we are alive, then we have done something wrong."

"Not at all, Diana!" she gently chided me. "There is no failure and there is nothing wrong in not meeting a personal challenge. Remember that all souls are in agreement of all challenges. In other words, you and Dodi agreed before reincarnating that you would not marry during that lifetime. So, Dodi did not fail within his own personal challenge; however, he did learn much. He recently told his spirit guide, Mondi, that he has finally learned while in the spirit realm why he and you died before you could marry.

"Just after his death," she continued, "when he was a newly-arrived spirit, he thought that something had gone terribly wrong because he did not fulfill one of his challenges to himself, which was to marry you. But, his guide reminded him that he and you both agreed that you would *not* marry. Dodi apparently had forgotten about that, but now, with this newfound knowledge, he is grateful for everything that happened within his life. He now knows that the accident was one of the greatest soul lessons he could have ever had because it freed his spirit once and for all from pointing the finger of blame at others. Of course, it took the level of forgiveness to remind him that he was never the victim but, in fact, the choreographer of this and every other lifetime he has ever lived."

I didn't reply immediately, but got up and started to walk along the shoreline of the healing ocean in order to contemplate what Ariel had told me. She let me walk alone to digest this information at my own pace. Being in heaven does not mean we suddenly understand all of life's mysteries or that we have all the answers.

I wondered why Dodi had to go to the level of hope. While alive, he was one of the most hopeful and optimistic people I had ever known. Why then, in death, would he not still be hopeful? Could he have taken our deaths as a personal failure? Why would he do that, though, when he'd had nothing to do with how we'd died? I thought back to where I had left Ariel and was instantly next to her again.

"I have followed your thoughts, Diana, and can answer them if you wish."

"Yes, please do, Ariel. I'm puzzled by what you said about what Dodi experienced on his arrival into heaven."

"Remember that I said that Dodi had needed to go to the level of forgiveness because he mistook your deaths as a personal failure and was harboring much anger?"

"Yes."

"Well, he needed to forgive himself, not others. You see, that is why he went to the forgiveness level first. He had to understand that not every challenge one sets up for oneself is even meant to be met. Sometimes the challenges are in themselves learning lessons. Once he was back in spirit, he had forgotten that the two of you had already decided that his personal challenge regarding your marriage would not be met."

"Oh, I do see now! What you're saying is that every spirit has both group and personal challenges to meet while alive? Well, I can see now why Dodi thought that he'd failed. He was getting his group and his personal challenges confused."

"Exactly! Dodi is fully aware of this fact now and that is why he is now relearning how to hope, because he had lost this very important ability when he was upon the level of forgiveness. When he was there, he told his guide that he would not hope or set difficult challenges for his next lifetime but that, instead, he would set up only challenges that would be easy to meet. At that, Mondi whisked Dodi off to the level of rainbows because a life without challenge does not lead to growth."

"That does so sound like my dear Dodi. He was always one to overreact at what he perceived to be a personal failure. He would often put his foot down and state very emphatically that he would never again do a certain thing or talk to a certain person if what he'd tried to do didn't work out. That's not to say that he was a quitter, but rather that he would not lower himself to beg or to complain about things not working out. He was quite independent and did not like the idea of accepting help from anyone."

"Yes, Diana, he was all of those things and so much more. He needs to see just how wonderful he is and what good qualities he and others have. You and he will not be reunited for some time because he has to immerse himself totally in his new learning and cannot be distracted."

Giggling, I asked, "Am I a distraction, Ariel?"

"Yes, Diana, Dodi is still in love with you and yes, at this time in his development, you would be a very major distraction indeed!"

"Ariel, will you let me know when I can see my darling Dodi again?"

"Yes, I will bring him to you when he has completed his learning. Now go on, Diana, to where you wish to be and send him your healing love and thoughts."

Ariel didn't have to tell me that twice! I loved Dodi in life as I love him in spirit. I sent him healing love and thoughts in abundance, and was very hopeful that we would soon be reunited to fly about heaven before he or I reincarnated.

I don't know if we will reincarnate together or not in our next lifetime, but no matter. He will always be a part of me and will be held within my heart forever.

Chapter 9

Fairies and Other Beings

D URING MY TRAVELS HERE, I HAVE FOUND THERE ARE OTHER spiritual beings apart from humans and angels. Often overlooked as spiritual beings are the plants, trees and animals, both domesticated and not. I will get back to the plants and animals in a moment, but at this time, I would like to share with you something that will surprise you. There is a group of lovely spiritual beings that I had always thought of as not real and found only in a child's story book. These beings are known as fairies. They are as real as the angels, and God created them to aid and assist his archangels and angels as they go about their appointed duties both in heaven and on earth.

The archangels have power and authority pertaining to everything upon the earth; however, they lighten their loads a bit by delegating some of their duties to the fairies. These tiny, twinkling creatures see to the day-to-day care of plants, trees and non-domesticated animals. At times, they will also be called upon to see to the needs of people.

Some of you have felt a light grazing of your ears, cheeks and necks. You could not explain this at the time because there was no stirring of the wind, no fans blowing or any draft. It may very well have been a fairy, possibly announcing to your spirit that an angel was on its way. Or it may happen when a person is not ready spiritually to accept information from an angel but will accept it soulfully from a playful fairy. However, the fairies in heaven as well as those upon the earth mostly tend to plants and animals. They fly about the animal or plant and administer to it with tender loving care. They heal what they tend only with permission from God, but wholeheartedly love everything that has been put into their charge.

All living things have a spirit within them that needs to be uplifted from time to time, as well as tended to regularly. When the spirits of plants leave the earth plane, fairies bring them up into heaven and place them all about. Here they will bloom forever as they gain a new magnificence to their beauty.

Animals, both domesticated and non-domesticated, are placed upon a level known as Utopia, or perfect world. They romp and play with one another, with the fairies and with the angels. They will never feel pain nor suffering again. Since neither plants nor animals have souls, they do not have learning lessons. There is no need for them to come back to the earth in order to live other lifetimes to gain experiences for their spirit's growth.

Non-domesticated animals as well as plants are given life mainly because of the ecological balances of the earth. They feed and cloth the earth's peoples, help to carry physical burdens, and irrigate and fertilize the soil. So, it would seem that every living thing has a purpose and a reason to be alive. All living things should be respected and cared for. This is where the fairies come in. They love to care about the things that people often do not have the time, or sometimes the inclination, to tend to. But the fairies and the angels know that people are not the only living things upon the planet and so they gladly go about their duties silently and joyfully fluttering about, tending the spiritual things of nature.

You may be thinking that the level of Utopia where the animal spirits are must be awfully crowded. However, keep in mind that in heaven the idea of space is meaningless. It is limitless in its capacity to house the spirits of the much beloved animals.

Domesticated animals that people love and have as pets are watched over by their own individual angels, as are people. Their purpose is to bring love, laughter, joy, and companionship into human lives.

Once a pet has departed the world, it can see its earth family from the level of Utopia. There are times when a pet's spirit wants to reincarnate back into the dear family it has recently left. This can be handled in any number of ways. For example, the pet's spirit may enter a newborn animal that the family will choose when they are ready to replace the departed pet. Or the spirit may enter into a newborn animal that "appears" to be homeless so that the grieving family will take in. The replacement animal may or may not be of the same breed as the one who passed, but no matter; it will have the deceased animal's spirit. Many people will recognize this spirit and remark upon the fact that the new pet acts very much like the old.

Animals have an enormous capacity to love and to give that love unceasingly and unconditionally. They also can sense and communicate with human spirits. Those animals that act mean, however, were not created that way but made so by the cruelties of people. Humans can be vicious and mean-spirited towards animals, and the poor creatures have no recourse but to snap and bite in order to protect themselves from future abuses. Some dog breeds, in particular, have been bred to be mean and aggressive. When these animal spirits arrive in heaven, they are placed on a healing level where angels and fairies work with them to heal their spirits before they take their place with the other animal spirits on the level of Utopia.

No animal is refused admission into heaven. They are all greatly loved because of their innocence and, for the most part, loving nature. Animals, like children, need to be taught how to behave. The best way to teach a child or an animal is with patience, firmness, love and respect.

Look upon all creation as a gift from God that will enrich and bless you, your lives and the planet, as well. Take care of the innocent things upon the earth. The universe is made up of every kind of being created by God. All things released in thought by a human spirit (excluding those of animals because they are not held accountable for their actions) are absorbed into the whole universe where they are stored. The conditions of your life are created from spiritual thought. If you are loving and kind within your thoughts, the universe will reflect that back to you and you will experience loving kindness more often than not within your life.

If you are cruel to an animal, it may not necessarily be cruel to you, but someone will be because that is what you have given out and that is what you must receive. In other words, what you give, you will get. Cruelty to animals does not go unnoticed by the angels, fairies or God. It is hard to say in what form or in what way the person meting out cruelty will have it returned, but rest assured, cruelty is often returned within the lifetime of the one who metes it out, oftentimes unexpectedly and almost always at a time when that person may be depending upon the kindness of others.

Those who have been cruel more than once will find themselves in a position of learning what an animal already knows— that love and care of the spirit and the body are essential for the survival of every species, man and animal alike.

Of particular importance are dolphins and whales, who have much to teach us. As most biologists and those who have studied them know well, these wondrous creatures are extremely intelligent. Dolphins have a gigantic capacity to love and to play. They, more than any other mammal, have an incredible ability to heal not only themselves when physically ill, but also people. If a disabled person were to be in the water with dolphins, one or two of the dolphins would come up the person and stay close to the affected area of the person's body. They would then transmit a special type of healing energy towards the area.

Doing this several times a week over a period of at least a month will bring about an amazing change in the person's condition. Of course, this is not suggested as an alternative to medical care, but why not also incorporate nature into healing, especially since nature is so willing and able to generously share its abundant healing knowledge with humankind.

Whales are the communicators of the deep. They have a finely-tuned intelligence that enables them to communicate not only with one another across vast distances, but also with dolphins and humans. These magnificent creatures are so much more valuable to the earth than most people think. They communicate with one another about the tides, ocean conditions, and impending natural disasters such as hurricanes.

These remarkable abilities are presently being studied but the research should be held in far higher esteem and advanced much more rapidly than is currently the case. The application and use of dolphin and whale intelligence in human lives is a vital necessity. People need to pay more attention to how it is that dolphins and whales have coexisted within the earth's oceans along with many thousands of other non-mammal species for millions of years. I might add that they have done this all rather healthily and happily. In other words, they help one another, they communicate with one another and yes, they love one another.

Applying and adapting dolphin and whale intelligence into human lives would prove to be an invaluable asset to mankind. For this reason, the slaughtering of these truly amazing, soulful, loving, air-breathing creatures should be banned and outlawed immediately. Through their superior telepathy and intelligence, they know what people are doing to them. These mammals of the sea pick up our thoughts and are desperate to understand why it is that people want to kill them not only for food, but often just for sport. And why we convene international gatherings to decide quotas of how many of each particular species various countries can kill in any one year.

Dolphins and whales are very much like humans in that they care for their young, have emotions that match and in some ways exceed our own, and in many ways are far more intelligent than humans. They want to be a part of the continuation of the planet as much as human beings do. Why on earth would destruction of these creatures be allowed when they have so very much to offer us? They wish only to give and all they ask in return is to be able to roam the oceans freely and without fear, and to live their lives upon this planet in harmony with humans.

Chapter 10

Relationships

RELATIONSHIPS ARE A PUZZLEMENT, ARE THEY NOT? THEY WERE for me and I assume they are for you, as well. Since being here, I have learned that we pick and choose those with whom we will interact within our lifetime, so you may be wondering why on earth you would choose to have in your life some of the dreadful people that you do.

Simply put, it is in order to learn and to grow. I realize that this sounds like a pat answer, but nonetheless, there it is. Knowing that you agreed beforehand to everyone and everything in your life may help you to understand and accept those who pose the biggest challenges to you. The very people who you see as a pain or a nuisance are really the best teachers you could ever have. After all, don't they sharpen your patience skills, increase your need for wisdom, and test the extent of your unconditional love?

Are you not thrown into self-examination in seeking ways of dealing with them more effectively? And maybe you are prompted to pray a bit more often. You will find that these are the spirits with whom you agreed, before you all incarnated, to be your mother and father, sisters and brothers, sons and daughters, uncles and aunts, and bosses, coworkers and neighbors. When you were in spirit form and setting up your life, you knew that you would learn nothing and gain even less if you chose to have only loving and adoring relationships. Where would be the growth in that?

Another important fact to keep in mind is that this is a two-way street. In order to promote the growth of those around you, you agreed to be a thorn in their sides, as well. You agreed to provoke them, stretch them, and make them look within to their spirit for ways of dealing with you. This in no way justifies any unloving act on your part, but it puts a different slant on things when you start to view yourself from the other's perspective. Perhaps in your prayers and conversations with your spirit, you could ask that you be less annoying to others instead of always asking that they be less annoying to you.

I hear protests from some of you right now defending your reasons why it is others who are in the wrong and how you are in the right. Again I say, for a moment, put yourself in their shoes, walk their walk, and live their lives. Just for a moment, hear them hearing you. See them seeing you. Do you understand why they feel and think the way they do? Know right now that you cannot change anyone but yourself. This truth should free you up quite a bit. If you start to change your outlook and your attitudes, you will see that others start to change in how they react to and respond with you. These changes may be slow in coming but, if you change, it is inevitable that others within your life will change, as well. After all, it is what you all agreed to do.

There is another point I would like to make that may surprise many of you. I have said that before you all incarnated together, you asked other souls within your soul group to play various roles in your life. Now in your soul group, you love one another deeply and dearly, and have done for eternity. Those souls who agreed to incarnate with you and cause you the most pain do so out of the deepest love for you and a desire to help you in your soul growth. Is it not ironic that those who hurt you the most are actually helping you the most out of the soul-level love that they have for you? For example, a boss or spouse who invalidates you and scorns you may actually be provoking you to look within yourself and summon up your inner power. You asked him or her to perform this valuable service for you so that you might explore issues around, say, personal power. On a soul level, you love each other without limit, and out of that love, agreed to live a life together of intense antagonism, as did Charles and I.

Please remember, also, that those spirits will also benefit when they return to heaven and must re-experience the hurt that they caused you. Through this, their soul in turn grows in understanding and wisdom. Again, this in no way justifies any unloving act because the whole point is to rise above such acts and arrive at a state of unconditional love for all.

The same exact principle holds true of your marriage and friendship relationships. You and the other spirits involved chose and agreed to incarnate together during a lifetime for the same reasons—to learn from each other and to grow. But what do you do about someone who steadfastly refuses to grow with you?

Earlier, I said that you may at some point within the relationship have to release those who do not in any way, shape, or form, honor or respect you. After ascertaining that this person, or in some cases persons, are not going to work towards having a positive and enlightened relationship with you, then it is up to you to release them from your spirit agreement. It is far better for your own growth to release someone with love from whom you feel only negativity than to continue dealing with them in ongoing rancor and malice.

To free yourself of people who are causing you no end of pain, hurt and humiliation and who are clearly not going to cooperate in the healing of your relationships, I will repeat how to go about releasing them from the spirit agreement you made. Whisper to your creator, to your angels and to your guides that you wish to release this person in love and peace. Thank them inwardly for upholding their part of your agreement, bless them and tell them that they are free to go, that they can no longer affect you at all. By doing this, you have freed yourself from their negativity and will not carry the weight of guilt or bad karma into any future incarnations you may have with any other incarnation of their soul.

It may take more than one time to fully release someone, but even so, when you do encounter them again even after your initial releasing exercise, you will notice that you no longer react to them or react less vehemently, and maybe even that you no longer feel anything, good or bad, about them, but as if you are meeting a perfect stranger.

People have relationships with every life-form there is. Think about the relationship that you have with your plants, trees and animals. Do you respect the fact that the plants, trees and animals of the earth have every bit as much right to exist as you do? The plants, trees and animals within your personal living space need, of course, water and nourishment. Do you supply those things? Do you place your plants where their faces can meet the sun? Granted, not all plants need or want the direct sunlight upon them, however, they still have specific needs in order to thrive happily. Do you meet those needs? By virtue of incarnating, you were vested with, and accepted responsibility for, the healthy and loving continuation of not only your species but for every species upon the earth. We are all of us, responsible for and to one another.

The most important relationship in your life will dictate how you, at this time in your development, relate to all of your other relationships. And what would you say *is* your most important relationship? Why, it is with yourself, of course. Your single most important responsibility is to love and honor yourself. Within this lifetime you have chosen to live, do not put yourself down, minimize your importance, or limit your power. Really get to know yourself. In other words, get totally honest with yourself.

Weed out all of the untruths that your well-intentioned but misguided early-life teachers told you about yourself, your gender, your race, or your "station" in life. All your teachers were doing was passing on what they in turn had learned when they were young. There is absolutely no reason why the cycle should repeat itself indefinitely, and I urge you to be the one to break it. Step out of the role that your society and culture have cast you in. Listen to your own spirit and follow *its* lead rather than old, outworn dogma about who society tells you that you should be.

Fully accept and embrace the fact that you are in the right place at the right time in this stage of your life and development. And if you are disillusioned or uncomfortable with any part of your life or relationships, you are being led by your guides and by your soul to acknowledge this truth and then to work through it.

Do not point the finger of blame towards others if you are unhappy within your present circumstance. You have the power and the resources available to you, twenty-four hours a day, to tap into in order to receive clarity and balance so that you can change and renew your life if you so wish. The power of your mind is immense. However, the power of your spirit is unimaginably greater than that of your mind.

What are these powers and resources available to you? They are, of course, your guides, angels and God, or whatever you call your creator. Once you tell them that you want and need them to communicate with you, they will do so. *But you must ask first* for they cannot simply barge into your life and start rearranging it for you.

Their reply is not always audible, although you might hear a still, quiet voice. It can be made apparent through dreams and through happenings that at one time you may have viewed as coincidences, such as when an acquaintance gives you advice or unwittingly suggests the perfect solution to your dilemma. Or, out of the blue, you may hear from someone who you've been thinking about but haven't seen for a while, someone who couldn't possibly have known anything about your situation, and yet that person's sudden appearance in your life helps you out tremendously by giving you the direction you need.

In the later years of my life, this happened countless times. People just magically "appeared" to give me exactly the piece of information or insight that helped me enormously in my growth and understanding. Of course, I went through some very dark years with no help at all, or so it seemed to me at the time. My challenge, of course, was to find and tap into my inner resources and not rely on my husband or my friends for my personal power and self-worth.

More important than anything I have previously mentioned, however, is the fact that your guides and angels communicate with you through your own thoughts and feelings. Your guides and angels talk to you all the time. Many times, a thought will come to you out of the blue that you know is not your own. When this thought is of a positive, good and helpful nature, you can be sure that it is from your guides. If, however, your mind is filled with negativity, it is not your guides speaking to you, but rather your own fears and prejudices that are surfacing.

The most effective way to release your fears and whatever other negativity you may have within is to simply say out loud a few times, "I am free of all negativity within me and around me."

I realize that this may sound awfully simplistic, but remember that your thoughts are powerful and that your spirit will recognize the good in what you are saying and honor it. In the beginning, you may have to restate your affirmation over and over to convince yourself that this is truly your desire, but even stating it for the first time, whether silently or audibly, will start to loosen the bonds of negativity within you.

In reclaiming your own self-esteem and freeing yourself from negativity, you are doing purely what you need to do for yourself. Keep in mind that when you begin to allow your guides to fully guide and instruct you, it is for *yourself* that you do this, and not as a means of changing anyone else. Once you begin to allow your mind to accept what your guides are saying to you and to let them become more actively involved within your personal decisions and opinions, you will inevitably see changes in others towards you. However, this is not because you have caused *them* to change, but rather because your change has encouraged their guides to nudge them towards *their* own personal growth challenges.

Spirit guides are of grace and politeness. They will never intrude upon your free will. Once you allow your guides to activate your true spirit, they will give you unlimited direction. You, however, must act upon this direction even though at first you may be apprehensive about doing so. Being accustomed to taking direction from others and not from ourselves, as I was from childhood, it may be difficult at first to listen to your own guides, but once you do, the rewards you will reap regarding your relationship with yourself and then with others will be boundless.

Finally, please remember that the relationships you have with others are direct reflections of the relationship you have with yourself. Other people are mirrors for you. Being surrounded with loving relationships points to a high degree of self-love. If you are plagued with unloving, even abusive relationships, I suggest that you examine your deepest feelings and beliefs about yourself. You have called those relationships to you as mirrors of what is in your own heart. Charles' total disregard for my well-being and his continued put-downs of my behavior were, if only I had known it, perfect mirrors for how I felt about myself at the time. Later on, once free of his negativity, I was able to form loving relationships and free myself of my own negativity. Then my self-esteem was unfettered and free to soar to wonderful heights.

What type of a relationship do you have with your creator? Do you talk with him, her or it everyday? Do you reflect upon why your creator made you in the first place? I call my creator God and, although while I was alive, I did not talk with him every single day, I did feel his presence at certain key times in my life. For instance, while I was walking down the aisle to be married, I heard in my head a voice that was not my own, but that of God. He told me that I should not marry if I felt at all apprehensive about it. I heard this over and over, and my own father even said those very words to me just before we started our procession down the aisle.

Being young and more than a little intimidated by the royal family, however, I thought that it would be easier to just get married than to face not only the royal family's disdain, but also that of the whole world. I chose not to listen to the voice of God and instead listened to the voice of fear. We all know how that ended up, don't we?

The other times in my life when I heard God's voice were when I needed to the most. It is apparent to me now that he spoke to me during the times when I was the most confused and frightened, just as a loving earthly father would do. He told me to do the most obvious things to free myself from my self-imposed chains. He advised me that I didn't have to do anything that I didn't want to do, that my first responsibility was to myself, that I was to look out for my own happiness and that I was surrounded by people who couldn't have cared less for me. However, hearing is one thing; listening is another, and I only started to listen to him about three years before I died.

I now know why I didn't listen to God's voice earlier. It was because I was unaware that it was, in fact, the voice of God speaking to me. I thought at those earlier times that it was my own doubts and fears crowding my mind and filling it with nonsense. However, I later found that it really was indeed God all along once I asked him to speak to me clearly and in such a way that I would know it was truly him. He did so by telling me in a dream that my heart, mind and soul had always been held by him and that fear was a figment of my imagination. He advised me to start living as if he and I were jointly in control of my life. I immediately put his suggestion to work in my day-to-day life and the results were spectacular, the changes nothing short of miraculous.

That is how I knew that I had indeed been instructed by God, my creator, about how it was that I could live happily and abundantly fulfilled every day of my life from that moment on. That is not to say that I didn't have my ups and downs, however, they were less frequent and much less severe in nature.

On the subject of relationships, I would like to talk a little about spirituality. All relationships are based in spiritual precepts or laws that you, in your spirit form, are quite aware of. It is the ego within you that desires for you to overlook or disregard these spiritual laws. While an ego is a good and necessary part of your being, it can, if not reined in, try to dictate to you what you should and should not feel, think or desire.

Your ego and your spirit are not on the same page. Your ego is driven only by human desires and wishes; your spirit is driven by the divine. So when your ego and spirit pull in opposite directions, they inevitably clash. To get your ego firmly under control, you must tell yourself that spiritual growth and knowledge will in no way demean or diminish you. You see, one thing that your ego does quite well and often to an extreme, is to protect the image that you have of yourself. Self-image is important up and to a point, but not when it takes over every area of your life.

One of the biggest challenges known to human existence is that of combining successfully ego and spirit. Some never succeed and that is why they come back again and again just for that purpose alone. It's too bad really, because there are so many other reasons to come back after you eventually get a handle on your ego that you unnecessarily increase the number of lifetimes that it will take for you to reach completion. Completion is when your spirit has encountered and successfully handled every condition put upon it throughout its many lifetimes. When your spirit has reached completion, it is then permitted to join with your soul in the presence of God all of the time.

To live successfully, you must allow your spirit to lead you, rather than just your ego. This is the truth as I know it to be, and as I said before, your experiences will differ from mine. I know however, that the basic principle still remains no matter what, and it is this: The spirit within you was not formed of fear but of tremendous knowledge, love and truth. It will shine brightly when you invite and allow it to.

Your spirit is the real substance of you. It will, along with your guides, advise you on your present relationships and your present misunderstandings of the world around you. Your spirit will talk to your ego once invited to do so, and tell it that there is no reason for it to fear the spirit. Once your spirit is leading you confidently throughout all of your relationships, as well as through all your life situations, you will advance that much further and faster along your chosen path and will have many more ups than downs. Life itself will make more sense to you, and you will find it to be so much more fulfilling. Once a hurdle has been managed, another will, of course, come up to take its place, but each successive hurdle will be far less work and far less challenging. And you will find that you are spiritually much more up to the task of handling it.

Lastly, I want to mention the great spiritual connection that children have from the time they are born until about the age of eight. While it is true that all spirits agree to come into a lifetime for the soul purpose of teaching and learning, your children are your best teachers and guides because they are still so connected with God and therefore with their source of spirituality. Little children see their angels and guides without fuss or fanfare. They accept these beings without question or fear because they have so recently just parted fully conscious company with them.

When you want to know truth in your spirit, look to a little child to lead you. Watch this child watch life. Follow a youngster about for a day and notice how he or she views every part of creation with awe and wonder. That is the true spirit within. In little children, there is no guile, no prejudice and no hatred. Watch how children of different races play together, unaware even of skin color, until some adult poisons their innocence. Again, only true spirit exists in the heart and mind of a child.

Of course, children have egos, too, and that is where you as the parent must step in to guide and correct your children into taming their egos. It is up to you to lead the children to understanding. Do so without beating or berating them, for when you do so, you tell them to incorporate fear, hatred and self-loathing into their spirits. How much more your lives would be enriched if you were to let your children be your teachers and your guides as you turned your attentions towards your spirit.

Let the little children tell you of their dreams, hopes and visions, for it is in those that they have spoken to their guides and angels. Put their drawings up on your walls, bless them and praise them for the pure love they give to you every day. Celebrate their goodness and uniqueness. Let them know that you are proud of who they are and of what they will become. Do not spoil them by giving them too many material possessions and other goodies, but do give them an unlimited abundance of your time, love and energy.

Children who are loved and respected by those with whom they are sharing a lifetime relationship will be continual sources of strength and blessing to each person they encounter within the family and within the community. I know this has been said before and I must say it again here: Your children are your future, therefore, bless them and invest your love in them. By doing so, you invite into your own lives untold blessings from your children's angels, from your own angels and, of course, from God.

Chapter 11

Life In Heaven

ARIEL AND I, ALONG WITH A SMATTERING OF OTHER SPIRIT GUIDES and angels, will address the questions that many of you have about crossing over and what it is that happens to you once you do. Keep in mind that, being individuals, different spirits will have somewhat different experiences. However, all will go through healing, various levels of learning and reincarnation studies.

Some spirits may have to undergo more intensive healing than others because they chose challenges that were extremely difficult to surmount within their lifetime. For example, a spirit may have chosen to be born into extreme poverty in a country that does not support the ideal of people rising above their class or station. This spirit may not even have made it to adulthood because of sickness, disease, being abandoned as a young, defenseless child without the aid of any adult caretakers, or living in a war-torn environment. This spirit will need special attention to assure it that it did not fail in its chosen lifetime, but that perhaps it was not as prepared for that lifetime as it thought that it was before incarnating.

Spirits who have incarnated upon the earth to explore one or more physical or mental disabilities receive full healing immediately upon crossing over. In their spiritual bodies, they are instantly whole and healthy. After a lifetime of physical immobility or difficulty, many run about wildly, leaping, dancing and laughing. So overjoyed are they that many will try to convey a message to their loved ones still on Earth announcing their new wholeness.

A spirit's guides will go over the lessons and all the good that the particular spirit brought into the world and review the people that it touched within its lifetime. You see, even if the lifetime was very short, no one lives in vain, and a spirit's life directly or indirectly touches everyone it encounters.

It is difficult to pin down an exact schedule or course of events that each spirit will go through, but I have assembled an outline of sorts that will pretty much sum up what you, yourself, can expect upon crossing over. Let me say further that some newly-arrived souls who had experienced an especially difficult lifetime will often say that they will never reincarnate again. That is acceptable, however they must still go through the studies of reincarnation to make absolutely certain of their choice. Of course, after studying about it, a spirit who has decided not to reincarnate may change its mind at some point further along within its evolution. That is why reincarnation studies are mandatory for all spirits.

Let's start at the beginning when you are just about to pass over. In those last few moments, and sometimes even hours, you will see your spirit guide. Now, a guide can either be a departed family member or friend, or even someone totally unknown. Further, you may not accept or trust the guide, whether known or unknown. In such cases, you may fight against either your imminent death or your actual death, as did my very dear friend Chris Farley.

If you do not have a clear idea of where it is you are off to, you may desire to stay back and quite astonishingly, pretend that you are either not dying or not dead. Your guide will try to convince you to come along and leave your earthly home behind. However, some spirits are so filled with fear of the unknown that they refuse to go. This is why some earth-bound spirits haunt, if you will, their earthly dwellings.

Once you walk into the light, which is a doorway into the heavenly dimensions, you will be met by your guides who will explain to you more than once that it is time for you to leave behind the dense negative energy. Even so, some spirits are still reluctant to leave their body or, if they already have left their body, reluctant to leave the earth plane behind. If the spirit refuses, it's guide leaves it alone for a while.

There are people alive today who can help earth-bound spirits to cross into the light, but these people must be careful because some spirits will actually lash out physically towards these helpful people and possibly harm them. A frightened earth-bound spirit is very much like a frightened animal—it scratches and claws at its rescuers because it is bound up tightly within its fear.

Fear in the human and animal spirits is an absence of knowledge. No living thing can go forward when it clings to ignorance. Animals have the excuse of limited brain function, but humans have no such excuse. Why, even those born with limited brain function go happily and lovingly with their guides. I was dismayed to learn that some spirits would rather stay upon the earth than go with their guides into heaven. These spirits can plainly see the light, and in order to go onwards, they must enter into it, which they can do at any time. I couldn't understand why a spirit would refuse the light. Stubborn refusal to go onward was a source of great puzzlement to me, so I asked Ariel, "Why would someone resist the light?"

Ariel, bless her, replied, "It is the spirit's will to stay or to leave, Diana, not the guide's.".

I asked Chris Farley why he had chosen to take his guide's hand and come into heaven, even though he had not wanted to leave the earth. He told me that his guide had been very tough indeed with him and had told him, "You must go. Now!"

Chris said that he had not realized that he had a choice in the matter. Some guides, like Chris Farley's, are quite convincing and leave no room for argument. Still, it was not Chris' guide who made the choice for Chris but rather Chris himself, even though he was not aware of it at the time.

So now the spirit has come into heaven. As it looks around, it will notice bright colors and amazingly beautiful scents and perhaps angels and previously departed loved ones or favorite pets. Ariel brought me into heaven and stayed with me for quite some time, talking and just being with me. After that time with Ariel, my healing began. I did not see anyone but her on and off for a very long time. I did notice very bright colors and beautiful scenery, but no angels. So you see, as I said earlier, everyone will have a slightly different experience. I was sent to the healing levels first, not because my lifetime had been so terribly difficult, but because, before I could be fully integrated with all of the other souls, I needed to release a tremendous amount of anger and self-anxiety that I had carried within me since I had been a little child.

Some spirits, however, for whatever reason, may be reluctant to release the anger or even hatred that marked their recent lifetime. They will experience a hell of their own making in which they may be joined by others with the same intent, each one amplifying the anger and hatred of the others. They can choose to stay locked in their loathing and self-loathing for as long as they wish, but they will not be healed until they choose to forgive themselves and whatever made them so vengeful during their most recent lifetime. The period of time they take to explore their self-imposed hell is entirely up to them.

For clarification, let me bring Ariel in at this point.

"I am Diana's spirit guide. I will explain about the differences between spirits and souls. A spirit is that which is breathed into humans, animals and all other things of nature by the creator through the soul. I call this creator, 'God.' The spirit inside of a person allows him or her to feel everything there is to feel. When your heart pounds with excitement and anticipation, it is your spirit hopping from foot to foot in anticipation. When you are overjoyed and you laugh and/or cry with delight, it is your spirit leaping within you. When you feel you cannot take another step, nor go on another day, it is your spirit that is weighed down by the burdens and demands that have been placed upon it. However, the ability to look up and see the sun shining again is also the spirit within you and it is always so.

"Your spirit functions entirely upon its own and is not controlled by your mind. Although your spirit is alive within you, it does not have the same world view as your mind does. In other words, your spirit tells your mind to rejoice and to live fully, no matter what your current conditions may be, but whether or not your mind listens is another matter altogether. You see, your ego is also talking to your mind, as well. Ego and spirit are two very different energies. Your ego is important and should not be put down. However, sometimes it can get the better of you and actually get in the way of your spirit. Your spirit will never dictate to your mind, but your ego most certainly will.

"This brings us to another energy within you—pride. Pride is fed from the ego, and both are essential within every person and animal, but like anything else, can get out of hand by becoming the sole reason why you are alive at all. The ego is actually stronger than pride. Ego dictates and rules pride; pride cannot overrule the ego. Pride knows that it cannot exist without the ego. They need one another and so there is never a fight between them.

"So, we have spirit, mind, ego and pride, and all are important and very much needed by every person alive. The trick is to allow the spirit—not the ego or pride—to lead the mind. How can you tell the difference between spirit, ego and pride? Easily. Your spirit will never tell your mind to do or say anything that will hurt or put down another, but your ego and your pride will, and often do. Your spirit will always look at the bright side of every situation, no matter how dire. Your spirit will bow to another. Think about how many times your ego and pride will do that?

"Spirit knows it is eternal and alive. However, the ego and pride grasp and claw at life because they know that they are not eternal. When the spirit of a person crosses over into heaven, the ego and pride within them do not. I want to make clear here that it is not your ego or pride that keeps your spirit earth-bound after death. It is your free will that does that. Your spirit houses your free will. So, if your will is to stay behind and not follow your guide into heaven, your spirit will obey.

"The soul is the life force of every person. To simplify, the soul is the engine and the spirit is the gasoline. One cannot work without the other but, the soul is really the dynamics of who and what you are. It is you. Take away the body and you have the spirit and soul. Your spirit and soul communicate all of the time. They are in perfect harmony with one another. Problems arise when you lose touch with the fact that your spirit and soul are having a human experience. When your ego allows itself to get so caught up within the world that you no longer think of your spirit, you no longer feed your spirit and you lose your way. A spirit needs to be looked after. It needs to be fed good spiritual books, to be in gatherings with other like-minded souls and most importantly, it needs to be able to talk openly and honestly with its creator through prayer. When these things are made available to your spirit, both your spirit and soul will blossom and grow within you, filling you with untold happiness and peace."

"I am Nathan, a spirit guide in charge of the scribes and the head of the reincarnation level. I will explain as fully as possible what reincarnation is about and the processes that are involved with it. To avoid the redundancy of using the words 'spirit' and 'soul' in describing a person, I will use the word 'spirit' only. Of course, your spirit and soul are part and parcel and cannot be separated, but I have taken liberties here for practical reasons.

"As the spirit goes through its levels of healing and learning, it has many opportunities to review its past lifetime. This review consists of first being placed by itself where it has nothing else to do but to go over how it handled the experiences and reactions it had towards the people, places and events that were a part of its life.

"This is definitely the most difficult part of the after-life process since many spirits do not want to face what their responsibilities were towards themselves and towards others while they lived. They want to say that things happened to them and that they were merely innocent victims, cast into roles they did not ask for. This is said in ignorance, because the spirit has not yet begun to access the spiritual knowledge it had before it incarnated.

"After a short while, however, this previous knowledge will be released fully and openly to the spirit from the soul and then real healing can begin. This is the only time that the soul speaks louder than the spirit. Normally, the spirit of a person is what is heard and felt, but in the heavenly realms, the soul takes precedence over the spirit. All knowledge is held within the soul and so the soul feeds to the spirit the information it has stored.

"While the ego falls away upon the death of the body, the person's free will does not. A person's free will has a life of its own and can be quite stubborn when it accompanies the spirit upon crossing over. It takes time for free will to quiet itself down so that the soul can tell the spirit what it needs to know.

"Free will, more than any other thing God gave to people, is what a person is really all about. Ego and pride are governed by the free will of a person. This may be shocking to many because it means that you freely hate, you freely hurt others and you freely hurt yourselves. How much more convenient it is to say that your ego made you do it, or that your pride got in your way.

"The reason why people are given an ego and pride is so that they can feel good about themselves and their accomplishments. However, this gets twisted and warped in some individuals whose free will tells their ego and their false sense of pride that the sun, moon and starts revolve around them.

"Outside of the body, free will does not need any other vehicle such as ego and pride to express itself. Most newly crossed-over spirits, except for a very few highly evolved ones, will have their free will acting as if the ego and pride are still active within the spirit. What has happened is that free will has forgotten that it does not need ego and pride to exist. That is why it can take, in human terms, a long, long time for a spirit to reach completion. It normally takes many, many incarnations for a person to fully incorporate all three parts of their being into one—free will, spirit and soul.

"When a spirit's guide puts the spirit on a level of contemplation or aloneness, the free will within that spirit will often refuse to examine the life just lived. Instead, it will want to do just about anything else it can, which is nothing at all really, because there are no diversions upon the contemplation levels. After a time, the spirit will realize that it had best get down to business, otherwise it will not be going anywhere until it does.

"After the lifetime has been reviewed, accepted and understood by the spirit, its guide comes back for it and takes it off to another level of learning. The next level depends upon what the spirit must next work out. It's all done in accordance with the spirit's needs.

"The first level, or levels, are to do with self-acceptance. On the next level, the spirit reviews its acceptance by other people of who it was in its lifetime and what it was that those people had to teach the spirit. Third, some spirits need to go to a forgiveness level where they must first forgive themselves and then forgive any others who have done any wrongdoing to it.

"The forgiveness level is most common for spirits who have been murdered or repeatedly brutalized within their lifetime. Here the spirit will have to face the fact that it agreed to the conditions of its past lifetime and, before it can move forward, it must know and understand that it cannot hold anger or malice towards any other spirit that had anything to do with its life, or death, as the case may be. The spirits upon this level come to understand eventually that they agreed to the circumstances of their lifetime in order to learn, to teach and to grow. You may argue that you would never have agreed to the harsh conditions that are a part of your life. However, whatever your individual conditions are, they have much to teach you if you remove your emotion from them and look at them as an objective observer would.

"Think of yourself as an objective observer for a moment. Once you have put some distance between your self and your situation emotionally, ask yourself what it is that you are learning or have learned by what you are going through or have gone through. What would you do differently and why haven't you done so already?

"Don't forget, you have a free will and it is not so very difficult to connect your free will with your spirit and soul. Tell yourself that you want to communicate with your inner being, and you will. This is not complicated or difficult. What is difficult, however, is having the ability to listen openly and honestly to what your spirit and soul have to say to you. Do not let your ego and your pride hush your spirit and soul. Tell yourself that, of your own free will, you will hear your spirit and soul out. Listen and learn, and then do as your heart leads you. Do not act in anger; act in love. Love and honor yourself, and then you will find that you can love and honor others.

"Some spirits go to a healing level after their self-acceptance levels. Here the healing angels work with the spirit to enhance its ability to hear its soul and guides more completely. Once this is done, the spirit goes onwards to various other levels of growth and learning. Some of these levels are creative levels where the spirit does nothing but create or learn to create; music levels where the spirit may choose to write music as well as listen and dance to music; play levels where the spirit does nothing but play in whatever way it chooses; reading levels; adventure levels and any sort of level that the spirit would like to be upon.

"When a spirit feels it is ready to reincarnate, its guides bring it to the level that I am on. Here it will meet with a scribe, with me and with its guides in order to go over all of the previous levels to see how much it has retained and to gauge its readiness for reincarnation. If they think it is ready to incarnate again and has mastered adequately the knowledge needed by its soul, I will then take the matter up with the spirit's creator.

"Once it has been decided that the spirit can reincarnate, its guide goes off with it to contemplate what the purpose of this new life will be. The spirit and soul will decide what knowledge it will bring to the new lifetime and what knowledge it will seek during it. This is when the spirit agrees to have certain conditions within its life, such as whether it will be born into wealth or poverty, with beauty or homeliness, in a positive or negative environment, with great love or limited love and so forth. It will choose its skin color, gender, the location of its birth, its parents and so forth. It will also meet and chat with the other spirits who will also share a large or small portion of its lifetime, and how and in what way the other spirits will affect it.

"Once all has been decided, the angels will carry the spirit into the womb of the female who will give birth to the new baby boy or girl. As you can see, reincarnation is a complex and deeply involved step and one that is never taken lightly. You planned your life in great detail while you were in spirit, so now that you are in human form, live it successfully and triumphantly by asking your spirit and soul to help you remember just what it is you came here for."

"I am Archangel Michael, and I, along with the other archangels, Uriel, Gabriel and Raphael, have power and dominion over all the earth. We were created to serve God's children. We do not want you to worship us, we do not want to be adored or revered by humans. We were created to do God's will. We love mankind and joyfully go about our appointed duties in serving and loving people. My name means, 'who is as God.'

"I am in charge of protecting and defending people. It is not so much that I protect you from what you can see, but rather from the things you cannot see, such as from the darker spirits and angels who seek to hurt and destroy what God has made.

"Uriel, whose name means 'fire of God,' is in charge of the earth itself, the things that grow upon it and the seasons. He purges the earth of disease and renews it, working with the sun and the moon to accomplish his duties.

"Gabriel, whose name means 'God is my strength,' has dominion over the waters upon the earth. She, along with Uriel and Raphael, have raised human consciousness over the past several decades by creating the desire in people to take a more active role in the conservation of the earth.

"Raphael, whose name means 'God has healed,' is the archangel whose steady hand guides doctors of surgery, whose healing words guide psychiatrists and psychologists as they counsel their patients, and whose wit and charm has uplifted and healed many.

"All of us influence what you perceive as important to the world and to the people within it. The movies and books that touch you, energize you and motivate you are placed into the thoughts and dreams of their creators by us. We seek out people who are open and loving towards all of mankind. We work closely with them, guiding and directing them step-by-step as we teach, heal and love through them.

"When we see a soul that is hardened against mankind, we do not interfere unless told to by God. We understand that this cruel individual also has a role to play within its lifetime. For every positive, there is a negative. For every good, there is an evil. It cannot be otherwise because heaven has not been brought down to earth yet. Once that happens, there will be no more pain nor suffering upon it. This will happen when God decrees it. In the meantime, know that you are all greatly loved by many within heaven. Your deceased loved ones, along with God and all of the angels, watch over you, pray for you and guide you daily. You can hear all of us within your hearts anytime you wish."

I am glad that so many were willing to impart heavenly knowledge upon all of you. I myself have learned and grown in so many ways while I have been here. A part of that growth for me has been to learn that I don't know it all and that I don't know enough yet in order to come back and live successfully. There is still so much I do not know. I need more time to be at peace and to chat with Ariel about the many options I have regarding my next lifetime. I am still getting in touch with my soul's knowledge. I find that it is far deeper and richer in more areas than I could have ever imagined.

Ariel has told me that she will continue to guide and direct me while I am here and even when I live on the earth again. I am glad for that. I trust and love Ariel deeply.

I spend my time here in contemplation of what I want next for myself, in watching how the angels perform their tasks, in learning how to do all sorts of various activities like walking on water, for instance, and sometimes I just revel in the sanctity and bliss of this place.

There is so much more to heaven than can be told; it is endless in so many ways. There are millions of parts to it that I have not even seen yet. I will see and do it all however, before I reincarnate. Heaven is limitless and far more expansive than anything that I can compare it to regarding earthly living. The reality is that the heavenly dimensions are far superior to the dimension inhabited by living people. The realms in heaven will never grow overcrowded or become too small to hold all of God's dearly loved souls. The concept of space is meaningless in heaven—the dimensions are simply never-ending.

There are other parts of the heavens that we as spirits cannot and do not access. God, being the supreme being that he is and the creator of these other heavens, has not revealed in detail to any human spirit just what these other heavens are for or who inhabits them. Human spirits inhabit a heaven that very much resembles the earth, except of course that it is purer and much more vast than the earth is. In cases of mass deaths, such as natural disasters in which thousands are killed, the souls of the deceased are met by their guardian angels and spirit guides just as a single death would be. There is no need for "reinforcements" to be called in because everybody has their own angel and guide.

Many of you wonder about what it's like on this side, for example, whether spirits have sexual feelings. Once a spirit has gone through all of the levels necessary for its healing and learning, it will join all the other souls and then it will have the constant feeling of being totally and wholly in love. It will find that it is like being embraced in the arms of a beloved and never being let go, quite happily, I might add. It is the soul's ultimate fulfillment. The feeling is even better than when you are ravenous and have your very favorite meal served in great abundance.

Many times throughout what you would call a day, every spirit, including plant and animal spirits, comes together to worship and to praise God for his wonderful goodness, love and mercy. When this happens, overwhelming happiness, ecstasy and love fill every inch of every being in heaven. Fireworks explode and flowers erupt in music that is more beautiful than anything ever heard upon the earth. After I experienced so much of the joy of heaven, I used to wonder why we can't remember all of this at the times of our lives when we need to desperately. But, I suppose that if we did, we might find our earthly lives even more unbearable than they may already be. It is for the best, then, that people don't remember every little detail of heaven but your spirit and soul do possess a wealth of heavenly knowledge that will guide, uplift and inspire you. Just ask.

You may wonder whether we on this side are aware of what is happening in the world we have left. Let me set the record straight. We are fully aware of daily events in the world, and are no less touched by them than are you. A good example is the publication of a book that purports to portray Charles' so-called side of our story. It is so easy to defame the dead, don't you think? If I were upon the earth and heard these ludicrous accusations for myself, I would, of course, be able to defend myself and rightfully put an end to these falsities.

The author of the book reports that Charles claims that I had plotted to kill Camilla. Admittedly, while I was alive, I had often wistfully hoped that Camilla were dead, and even though I was not known for my quick mind, I was not stupid and most certainly did not plot to have Camilla killed. Of course, words can be misconstrued and that is obviously what has happened here. Charles is trying to turn the tide of public opinion in his favor so that those people upon the earth who still love and honor me and my memory will be hoodwinked into thinking that Charles is being up front and honest. The poor dear still does not realize that he is out of his league. I'm sorry if that sounds a bit snide and persnickety but I am answering for my soul's honor, not from or for my ego.

If I were alive, I would be bingeing and purging over these ridiculous outright lies and the sheer vileness of my ex-husband's words. It upsets my sense of right and wrong terribly and causes me enormous stress that my children are being made miserable by this whole mess.

Charles is being honest about one thing, however—he did feel a tremendous sense of relief regarding my death, but only after the initial shock wore off. When he walked so somberly behind my body, he did feel remorse. Of that I am certain. I was there in spirit and I know beyond a shadow of a doubt that he was not acting or putting on.

My concern for my children's emotional and mental wellbeing supersedes even that of my honor. A multitude of angels and other spiritual beings here in heaven will see to it that my children are protected from any further harm. This is not an idle threat by any means. When a departed spirit such as myself is in despair over loved ones, all of heaven converges upon the hearts and minds of those who are suffering. While my children will not be magically lifted up and away from their strife, they will be given a richer spirituality and other ways and means with which to get through their trying times. A deeper sense of compassion towards all of mankind will be theirs, and once they are grown completely, they will make decisions that will affect their father in ways that he can hardly imagine. Their angels are with them constantly, comforting and healing them on a daily basis.

Charles and Camilla continue to leave a trail of bitterness and tears behind them as they trample upon my memory. However, one day they will have to walk upon that trail themselves and reap the rewards of their wasted efforts.

Dear William and Harry, do not despair, for my memory will stay alive and intact in the hearts of not only you, my dear ones, but also in the hearts of all those who truly loved me.

It is time for me to go on now. I wish you all joy, happiness and so much love upon your journeys. Look up into your night skies and notice a bright, twinkling star. Know that I am sending you light and love upon your path. Thank you for allowing me to share my journey with you.

I wish you all courage, truth and tremendous love forever,
Diana

Epilogue

In closing, I would like to ask that you not consider the source of these words remarkable. From my vantage point, it is normal that those on a higher dimension communicate with those still in physical bodies. So please do not be distracted by the fact that it is I, Diana, speaking to you.

Instead, please focus on my message: that the realms we inhabit before and after death are one, separated only by a thin veil of perception. When we are born, we accept a limitation in conscious perception in order to focus on whatever challenges and growth we intend for that lifetime. If it weren't for that limitation, we would not be able to dedicate ourselves to the tasks at hand on the physical plane. However, when death frees us from those limitations, we return once more to our larger perception and continue growing. Therefore, please do not mourn my passing since I for one certainly do not. In fact, to those of you who have lost or will lose someone close to you, please remember that they are not lost at all, and are constantly with you. Also, when it is time for them to move on in their growth, your mourning will hold them back from what they must do. The saying, "If you love something, let it go," was never more true than in this case. Cherish their memory by all means, but do not tether them to the physical plane by your grief.

Instead of mourning the dead, please celebrate their liberation to the higher dimensions, much like a parent celebrates when a child is ready to leave home and start life as an adult. The parent may miss the child, but knows that he or she is fulfilling whatever destiny has been chosen. It is a cause to celebrate the passage to adulthood, just as death is a cause to celebrate the passage back to spirit.

My main message to you, therefore, is to prepare during your lifetime for the continued growth that follows death. Endeavor to live a life as full of as much love as possible, and as free of guilt, blame, anger, and hostility as possible, because those traits will hamper your smooth progress in the higher dimensions. You will have to deal with the discord that you caused to those around you before you can continue your growth on this side. When Jesus said, "Be ye as little children before you can enter the kingdom of heaven," what he was saying was, strive for childlike innocence, unconditional love, and awe of creation, then your growth and expansion can continue over here without missing a beat.

I see clearly now that physical life is not meant to be full of struggle and conflict but is an opportunity to practice unconditional love for yourself and those around you. The only struggle in your life is what you put there by resisting the force of love in the universe, by not knowing that you are a soul having a human experience, and by choosing to believe that you are not an integral part of God—whatever you perceive that to be.

For those who have difficulty loving yourself, I only wish you could see yourself as I see you—a bright spark of God-ness. Faith is the acceptance, without having any tangible evidence, that you are a spark of the divine. It is seeing the "God-spark" in yourself and others when the world around you, even organized religion, is telling you otherwise.

And finally I would urge you to nurture the little children and heed their words, for in a sense, they are closer to the truth than are most adults, because they are more recently separated from the spiritual realms where all these truths are known and taken for granted. Please do not beat these beautiful truths from their tender awareness but foster it, for the future is in their hands.

God bless to you all, Diana.

About the Author

At the age of six, Christine Toomey was visited by her mother in an After-Death Communication (ADC). Her mother, who had passed away when Christine was three, told Christine that she was blessed with a most wonderful gift—the ability to see and to hear spiritual beings—one that was to be used to help and to guide not only herself, but others, as well.

When Christine was 20 years old, she began to use her psychic abilities, tentatively at first but soon in earnest. Time and again, clients told Christine how much her advice and counsel had helped them and she made the commitment to herself, her mother, and to God to be an open and receptive channel through which spiritual energies could flow.

The results of that commitment have been an outpouring of spiritual communication from not only Princess Diana but from Chris Farley, John Lennon, John Candy, John Belushi, Jesus and Mother Teresa, to name only a few.

Working with angel energies, spirit guides and other spiritual energies for over 20 years, Christine has helped and counseled thousands. She conducts lectures and workshops and is a frequent guest on radio shows throughout the U.S.

She makes her home in Charleston, South Carolina with her husband and three sons.